The Sisterhood folios

F*CK
FEAR

living a courageous life

Creative
PUBLISHING GROUP

Acknowledgments

Ruth-Anne Boyd

I dedicate this book to my amazing sons: Matthew, Brandon, and Michael. You taught me how to love unconditionally. You inspire me every day to be the best mom I can be. Thank you for that! I am extremely proud of each and every one of you. To my incredible husband, Randy, who keeps me balanced and calm, and helps me to stay strong no matter what is thrown at us. You are my rock and I don't want to live a single day of this wonderful life without you. Thank you for standing beside me for the past 35 years and here's to 35 more. I love you with all my heart. Finally, to my dad, Lyle, who was my hero. I miss you more than words can say. Rest in peace now dad. I'll take it from here.

Amy Brasier

I would like to thank my family and friends for all their support through good times and hard times especially my children that make the sun always shine brighter, their big hugs and pushing me through, including my fur babies, that never really understand, but love me unconditionally. A special thanks to my love and partner in crime for his support in my health battles, I know it is never easy to deal with someone like me, let alone hold my hand on my life journey! I love you all and blessings to you..

Kimberly Carson-Richards

First to my husband, Regan, thank you for your never-ending love and support. To my son, Jon, I am so proud of the man you have become. To my daughter, Mikaelyn, your unlimited joy and enthusiasm inspire me to be a better person. To my mother, Marie, thank you for being there for me whenever I needed help. To my dad, Don, who I only found and met

2 years ago, our conversations always make me feel happy! To my daughter-in-law, Kailey, thank you for being part of our family. Thank you to my friends and family members for your love and support. Lastly, a special thank you to Carol Starr Taylor for giving me the opportunity to share my story of courage in her Sisterhood Folios series.

Shawna Flinkert

To my partner Marc for being my rock on the days when the rivers of tears are flowing, or the days that silence is my armor. For your ability to make me laugh and cry at the same time. For being my greatest supporter and knowing when to give me that much needed nudge. I love you.

To my stepson Jack for being the most positive person I have ever met. Your ability to always see the world with rose-colored glasses while living with a chronic health condition is beyond words. You are a true inspiration to those around you.

Emlyn Jackson

Thank you to the ambitious, heart centered person who is ready to share the hidden rewards of their ugly truths.

To my parents and siblings: No matter how far away we are from each other, I appreciate your continued love, patience, and support. You are forever in my heart.

To my beautiful daughter, you are my #1 inspiration. I admire your brave heart and kind soul. Thank you for your unconditional love and understanding.

Rico, thank you for your enthusiasm and motivation for life. Cheers to many more adventures!

Carmela Lamanna

I can't help but feeling overwhelmed with gratitude! I miss my parents every day, I am one lucky woman for having the family who understands and supports me. To my husband whom I love unconditionally, I will always be grateful for the freedom and support you have shown me, we have fought some fearful situations together and we have both grown so much by them, we have raised two beautiful strong daughters that we couldn't be more proud of, now we are watching our grandchildren grow, with so much pride in our hearts.

Michele Anne Lopaschuk

To all the powerful woman that have come into my life and have shown me endless inspiration, guidance and encouragement throughout my journey.

I'm very grateful and want to thank you all for believing in me. Special thanks to my empathic Counselor Henny deLange, my empowering Managers, Diane Baird, Leslie Martin, and Katharine May, my supportive Colleague/friends, Debbie Nelson, Lucy Urquhart, and Martina Breunig, my nurturing Facilitator, Gail Robertson, my motivational Coach, Zoe Zlatoslava Petrak and my influential Business Partner, Dianne Solano.

Most importantly, I wish to thank my kind-hearted friend, Stella Paniccia who helped me with writing my story.

Jasmin MacKinnon

To my mom Denise, thank you for starting the healing process of changing our legacy to a healthier, happier one. Your grace and strength is undeniable.

To my sister Leelee, my beacon, thank you for loving me unconditionally and holding me always.

To my amazing husband Adam who's shown me the unimaginable; true love and unwavering support.

To my babies Aiden and Eliza, you inspire me to be a better Being. To Tina and Terra, thank you for being my cheerleaders, proofreaders, and sounding board.

To ALL of you who believe in me and 'see' me, I am eternally grateful.

Cheryl Martin

To the universe and spiritual karma for bringing me through the lessons and insisting I never give up on my own growth. To my daughter Silvia, who is my heart and the fire underneath me to clean up the past. For you I break the patterns. To my family, for supporting me, forcing me to grow and never actually saying "I told you so." To my coaches, mentors and my community of coaches, entrepreneurs and Soul Circle: for seeing my magnificence even when I could not, for pushing me off the cliff and allowing me to soar.

What you resist, persists. So I persist, until it ceases to exist.

Nadine Matejuk

I dedicate my chapter to and thank these incredibly special people in my life:

Thank you to my beautiful daughter for giving my life meaning. I am so proud of you and love you so much!

Thank you to my family for being my best friends growing up, keeping each other safe and for your love and strength over the years... Love you always!

Thanks to my friends for the laughs, chats and having my back without judgment.

All of these people make my life complete and that's pretty darn precious!

Love and Hugs, Nadine xoxo

Janice Pavicic

To my husband who is my light, my rock, my soulmate. You helped me find my way through the darkness and through to the other side.

To my daughter who is my heart. I love you with everything I am.

To my Mom and Dad in Heaven, thank you for the lessons, till we meet again

To my little 6-year-old self, it will all be okay, you are strong, you can make it, you are loved.

Erin Pellow

"There is no joy without gratitude" Brené Brown. To my parents, thank you for believing in me when I didn't believe in myself. To Rebecca and Bryanna, for being whatever I need whenever I need it. To Robyn, for helping me to feel beautiful and letting me see the sun porch. To eLiz for asking brilliant questions. To my fellow CrossFit athletes at Northern Touch CrossFit, thank you for continuing to inspire me. To my coaches, thank you for helping me become a better athlete. Finally, to Erin and Darryl, for creating a community that truly supports us in living our best lives.

Julie Steeves Benson

Thank you to my daughter Shirra, my greatest accomplishment; who never ceases to inspire me with her extraordinary art and for providing me with two angelic grandbabies. For my friends and family, each like precious diamonds filling my world with sparkle, thank you for your support. Mother Earth, thank you for providing me with an extraordinary landscape to find peace and balance for my soul. Sincere thanks to all the dedicated volunteers that make each day a better place for the struggling and downtrodden. Bless you!

Mia Valente

To my close family members and friends in Canada, UK, Europe and USA. This is for you. Thank you for all your love and support.

Chauna Welder Leek

To my husband Steve - thank you for standing by my side through these very tough years.

To my parents - saying thank you is not even close to being enough. You have never left my side. I am forever grateful for the two of you.

To my bestie, Carla, who is always there encouraging me.

To my beautiful daughters Kamryn and Aidyn. Because of you, giving up was never an option.

Lastly, thank you to all of you who thought my story is worth sharing.

Table of Contents

Foreword by Lisa McDonald   13

Abandoned! by Ruth-Anne Boyd   17

My Fight To Survive by Amy Brasier   31

A Life Lived Fearlessly: The Tale of a Teen Mom
by Kimberly Carson-Richards   41

I Am Enough by Shawna Flinkert   57

Ugly Truth by Emlyn Jackson   73

Growing Stronger Through Fears
by Carmela Lamanna   89

Finding the Magnificent Michele
by Michele Anne Lopaschuk   99

Damaged Goods by Jasmin MacKinnon   111

Breaking Free by Cheryl Martin   127

In Charge Of Your Destiny by Nadine Matejuk   143

Breaking the Chains by Janice Pavicic   159

Just One Thing by Erin Pellow   173

Removing the Mask by Julie Steeves Benson   187

Sexy, Fearless and Fierce by Mia Valente   201

Fear of Faltering by Chauna Welder Leek   215

*When women put their heads together,
powerful things can happen!*

~Oprah Winfrey

Lisa McDonald

Foreword

"Uplifting you to fear less and to live more!"

F*ck Fear. And the women who shared their stories with us in this powerful book did just that. Faced with challenges, obstacles, physical and emotional abuse, accidents, illness and the always hovering 'fear' that unfortunately coincides with these adversities, they found strength and courage within themselves not to cower behind the oppressiveness.

When I was graciously approached to write the foreword for this book I was deeply honored. As a woman myself who is all too familiar with what it means to choose to rise, to overcome, to speak out, to relinquish fear, and to embrace self-love, self-forgiveness, and self-empowerment, I silently appreciated and loudly applauded the authors.

I am an incest survivor, someone who has been self-sufficient and on my own since the age of sixteen. Now a single parent to two young children, I have a very intimate relationship with pain and fear. Knowing what it has felt like to be directionless, alone, and without support for a good portion of my life, I was thrust into having to figure things out exceptionally fast.

The miraculous gifts, the lessons and the blessings I have received from all hardships endured in my life has afforded me the opportunity to authentically empower others to empower themselves. I have dedicated my entire career and life to working with the marginalized, the oppressed and the abused. I am forever committed to paying it forward and being of service to the collective in whatever capacity or vehicle is at my disposal. Staunchly immersed in the world of personal development and personal growth, knowing that there are unfortunately too many people like myself who could identify, and relate to my personal experiences. Like the stories we will read in this book.

These are real women, writing with a raw authenticity that comes from the heart. The words written with bravery yet at times blurred with the pain of memories. No filters, just heartfelt truths. We are ultimately left with a smile, as the victim rises to overcome, but it is a bittersweet smile, mingling with the tears overflowing from a journey of hopelessness and fear.

It's not an easy task, baring your soul, your pain, your fears... your reality for all to read. Exposing fully your emotions and thoughts, when fear has always bullied them into hiding. But these women, all of them, share their personal journey with us within these pages. By the end of each chapter we are left cheering.

Do all the stories end in 'happily ever after?' No. But definitely they are 'happily living fearlessly' and isn't that what we expect from such a meaningful title? These women looked into the blackness called fear and chose to not only say the words but live them... **F*ck Fear!**

Lisa McDonald is a successful Author, motivational speaker, TV and radio host, podcaster, blogger, mentor, personal development coach, and mother.
In 2017, Lisa became a blogger for Arianna Huffington's Thrive Global, a website dedicated to offering readers sustainable, science-based solutions to enhance both well-being and performance. Her podcast, Living Fearlessly with Lisa McDonald, can be heard on both C-Suite Radio and Contact Talk Radio Network. You can watch her television show, Living Fearlessly, broadcast online at 365TVNetwork.com. Lisa's first nonfiction adult book is scheduled for release May 2018, her first foray into non-fiction writing following the success of her four bestselling children's books: Little Boy Gan From Passion-Filled Everland, Reimburse the Universe, Planet Pome-Granite and Kismet Tales from Happy Trails. She is also a contributing author to several motivational bestsellers: 365 Moments of Grace, 365 Life Shifts, Thought Leaders: Business Expert forum at Harvard Faculty Club, and Shine Your Light: Powerful Practices for an Extraordinary Life. Lisa holds degrees from McMaster University and Mohawk College and is licensed as a Passion Test Facilitator. Lisa's personal and professional life are embodiments of her teachings; she is fiercely passionate about uplifting people to fear less and to live more
http://livingfearlesslywithlisa.com/

Life shrinks and expands in proportion to one's courage.
~Anais Nin

Ruth-Anne Boyd

Abandoned!

Tears rolled down my cheeks. My heart ached so much that it felt as though it was going to break into pieces. *Will I be ok? Who is going to look after me? Doesn't anyone love me anymore?* These were just some of the questions that frantically raced through my mind as I watched my mom pack up her belongings into a couple of suitcases, put them into her car, and drive away.

I was only nine years old that day when my mother decided to leave. She didn't just walk away from me though. She also left my dad. Worst yet, she left my baby brother who was only five years old on that heartbreaking day. After her car disappeared into the distance, there was really only one question remaining in my mind. *Were we being abandoned?*

There are certain things that people say to you throughout your life that you never forget. Sometimes, you don't get over them either. You know what I'm talking about. It's that one thing that someone said to you that you can't stop thinking about. You're not sure why. It just lives rent-free in your mind. I think about certain things that people said to me when I'm driving in the car by myself, left with my own thoughts. And, boy, do they stir up old feelings, ones that I guess I never resolved.

Thoughts are the shadows of our
feelings – always darker, emptier and simpler.
~Friedrich Nietzsche

There was one particular conversation that took place about 20 years ago that I can't seem to get out of my mind. During lunch with a friend we were talking about being moms and what that meant to each of us. My friend made a comment that some women who are born between May 29 and May 31 don't make very good mothers. At the very moment those words left her lips, I was shocked and, to be honest, I didn't believe her.

My mom was born on May 29. I would say that, in her case, the words my friend shared with me at lunch that day are true. My mom has never really been a very good mother. She abandoned her two children over and over while we were growing up. There is one big question remaining in my mind today. I have asked myself that question over and over for most of my life. *Why?* She brought us into this world. When you make a decision like that aren't you responsible for loving and guiding your children until they become beautiful and amazing adults? I certainly think so.

When my mom left me and my brother at nine and five years old, it really affected us. We were so very young. We were old enough to understand what was happening, but too young to be left on our own. Being the oldest, I had no choice but to put my big girl pants on and care for my little brother. It wasn't easy. I'm not going to try and sugarcoat it. At nine years old, I should have been hanging out with my friends. Instead, I was cooking meals, doing laundry, and cleaning the house, all on top of making sure my schoolwork was done.

My dad tried his best to be there for us after my mom left but it wasn't easy. He owned a convenience store and worked up to 16 hours a day, seven days a week. Needless to say, he wasn't home very much. We were scared. Left alone in the house pretty much all the time, we didn't felt safe. We ended up having to raise ourselves.

After only a few months of struggling to cope with two small children, my dad decided we needed more. More guidance.

More love. Just more. I truly believe he just wanted a better life for us when he took us to live with his cousin and her husband. Since they were much older than us, my dad decided we would call them aunt and uncle. Let's call them Aunt Jill and Uncle Jack.

I remember moving in with Aunt Jill and Uncle Jack like it was yesterday. Intense sadness and fear swept over my entire body that faithful day my dad dropped us off. It was heart-wrenching. I was so confused. With no one that I could talk to, I was left wondering why this was all happening. We didn't belong here. This wasn't our home. It was only a few hours before desperate feelings of loneliness began consuming my entire body.

Not belonging is a terrible feeling.
It feels awkward and it hurts,
as if you were wearing someone else's shoes.
 ~Phoebe Stone

One by one, the six children who lived with my aunt and uncle introduced themselves. I was shocked as they just kept coming forward. The house felt as though it was bursting at the seams. Nevertheless, my brother and I were about to make children number seven and eight.

To fit everyone into the small, semi-detached home we were stuffed into almost every corner and available space on every floor. The girls slept in bunk beds in some rooms while boys were housed in other rooms. I had never shared a room with anyone before so it felt odd to me. I wasn't sure that I could trust the other girls in my room. For the first time in my life, I began looking over my shoulder. I hid my important belongings between the mattresses to make sure no one stole them. After all, this was all I had left of my time with my parents. It wasn't long before I had to face my fears and be strong, for both me and my brother.

For two years, my brother and I lived with a family that wasn't ours. My dad came to visit as often as he could. It was hard for him to find someone to run his store. When he was able to leave for a few hours he made the 45 minute trip each way to visit us. When my dad wasn't there with us, my brother and I were lonely and afraid. We were desperate for more time with our dad. We needed a hug. We craved the kind of unconditional love that comes from your parents.

Living in the house that belonged to my aunt and uncle wasn't a fun place to be, to say the least. My brother and I were abused regularly but in different ways. He was mentally, emotionally and physically abused. I, on the other hand, was sexually abused over and over by my uncle. Uncle Jack was a very sick man. He sexually abused most of the five girls that lived in the house, but not everyone. Two of the girls were his own children and he never touched them. The rest of us were either stepchildren or distant family members and he sure had his way with us. Each night, when my aunt went to work as a nurse, he took turns with each girl. I imagine that he felt great power having the house all to himself and doing whatever the hell he liked.

The two years of repeated sexual abuse was life-altering for me. All of those nights of being violated, feeling absolutely terrified and never having the comfort of safety shaped the very adult I became. They made me feel as though I wasn't good enough. I believed that I was fat, even though I was only 120 lbs. for most of my life. I became intensely afraid of having any kind of relationship with anyone.

After enduring the circumstances in that house that never felt like home, the day finally arrived when my dad came to take us back home. I was eleven and my brother was just seven at the time. After what seemed like many hours in the car but in reality was only just under an hour, my dad didn't take us to the home we had known all of our lives. We arrived at an old, three-floor apartment building. It felt like such a strange place to me. It certainly wasn't home to me. To make matters worse, I now felt disconnected from my dad. I wondered how he could send us away to such an awful place for so long. It really felt as though I no longer had parents that loved me. I was lost.

When my dad opened the door to our new apartment I noticed my mom standing inside. I was shocked! My mind immediately began to race. *What is going on? What is my mom doing here? Is she just visiting? Should I tell my parents what really happened to us while we lived away from them?* No way, I thought. I can't share that kind of information with them. It would be awful. It would make them feel bad. It seemed that having to instantly grow up and take care of my little brother was turning me into the parent, even though I was only eleven years old.

As strange as it felt to see my parents back together, it was amazing to be a family again. Just like a warm blanket surrounding me on a cold winter night, I felt safe for the first time in a very long while. I felt cared about and loved. I developed a tiny glimmer of hope that, finally, I would have a family like everyone else did.

Those wonderful feelings that made me feel like dancing as if no one was watching didn't last long. My mom started having another affair, so my dad asked her to leave. My father wasn't the kind of person who openly shared his feelings with us. I think my dad wanted to protect us. His pain was obvious though. It was written all over his face. For me, watching my mother pack up all of her stuff, put everything into her car, and leave again without so much as a kiss on the cheek was excruciatingly painful. She was about to abandon us again!

An unfortunate pattern of nontraditional circumstances had now developed in my life. Lack of unconditional love and acceptance, as well as never feeling safe were taking a toll on me. I started believing that no one actually loved me. In fact, I didn't even really like myself very much. To make matters worse, the fact that I had never felt safe was causing even bigger problems. I no longer trusted anyone. I was afraid of being alone. I avoided dark rooms like the plague. And, I never went into basements. The very thought of doing any of these things would make me shake violently so I avoided them at all costs.

Now that there was just the three of us again, we had no choice but to go on with our lives. Since my dad wasn't around most of the time, as the oldest I felt compelled to step up again. As terrified as I was about the situation I now faced, and as much as I was struggling, I did everything I could for my little brother. From cooking to cleaning and making sure he always had clean clothes, I wanted him to feel safe. I wanted him to feel loved. Most of all, I wanted him to know I would always be there for him.

For most of my teenage years, neither my mom nor dad was around very much. When my dad was home, he was usually tired and angry. Unfortunately for me and my brother, he was raised by parents who believed in spanking their kids with a belt and cutting them down if they didn't act as expected. My brother and I were belted regularly. I remember one particular time when my dad became very angry with me for coming home 10 minutes late. He took me to the basement of our house and belted me until there was blood running down my legs. I screamed and cried uncontrollably but he wouldn't stop. My relationship with my father would never be the same after that day.

The physical abuse wasn't the only thing I endured as a teenager. My dad had a girlfriend who liked to emotionally abuse both of us kids. She would call in the middle of the night just to put us down and blame us for everything that was going wrong in her life. My dad allowed this to happen, over and over again. It was awful!

The physical and emotional abuse at home was like the straw that broke the camel's back for me. It caused me to disconnect from everything and everyone. I went through the motions of life but chose not to feel anything, so I wouldn't have to relive painful memories. I distanced myself from every family member and friend to make sure that no one else could hurt me. I existed but that was pretty much it. Things were bad at home. So bad that I wanted to leave as soon as I could.

With no inkling of what was happening to me and my brother at home, my mom just went on with her life. I heard through the grapevine one day that she had a new boyfriend who wanted to take my mom and move to another country. I couldn't believe it! I remember thinking that my mom was going to leave us again! And, she did. Just after I turned 17 my mom and her boyfriend moved to Australia. Off they went without so much as a phone call, hug or visit. This time, though, I couldn't bear to watch her leave. It was just too painful. I wished her a good flight during a quick phone call to her and off she went.

They say that abandonment is a wound that never heals.
I say only that an abandoned child never forgets.
  ~Mario Balotelli

When I stop to actually think about it for a moment, I get incredibly sad. I don't believe that my mom has ever really been happy. For as long as I can remember, my mom has been searching for that one person, that one guy, who would make her happy. I'm not sure she has ever figured out that happiness actually comes from within. You decide to be happy! For me, it's a conscious decision I make every single day after I wake up.

The very day that I turned 18 years old was a significant turning point in my life. I didn't even wait until the end of that day to make arrangements to move out on my own. I packed up my stuff, put everything into my car, and moved into an apartment with a girlfriend. My dad was devastated. I'm sure that was just his guilt talking after belting me for so many years. He ended up not speaking to me for months.

Once on my own, I got a full-time job and started really living. For the first time ever, I loved my life. I was finally free of all of the sexual, physical and emotional abuse. I think I even started to like myself again.

While at work one day, I noticed this gorgeous guy walking towards me. I was instantly mesmerized. It didn't take long before we started dating. He was the mail boy and I was the office secretary. We took long walks, talked for hours about life and our dreams, and even met up for a quick kiss in the stairwell at work. We fell in love. With someone special in my life, I finally had the security and love that I so desperately needed and very much wanted.

The beginning of the relationship felt amazing, pretty much like a fairytale. In only a few months, though, doubts about being good enough for him and worthy of his love started to creep into my mind. The repeated abuse was rearing its ugly head. Before long, I was afraid to be by myself. I needed constant reassurance that he loved me. I could only fall asleep if he held me. I didn't feel safe going too far from home so going on vacation was out of the question.

It took a few years for me to realize that these feelings weren't normal. Although I was head over heels in love, I was struggling with my own self-worth and that was getting in the way of having a deep relationship with him. I needed help. What I really needed was a therapist. So, I got one. What a gift my therapist was. She helped me work through all of my feelings, and accept a past that I could not change. It took many sessions with her but I now know, without a shadow of a doubt, that it's ok to ask for help. Sometimes, we just need to talk to someone.

My boyfriend and I dated for more than five years before he asked me to marry him. I believe it took that long because I was damaged when we first met. I honestly couldn't start a new life before I dealt with my past.

Just before I turned 25 years old I called my mom to let her know I was getting married. She broke my heart when she told me she wouldn't come to my wedding. I took some time to accept that my mother wouldn't be there to see me walk down the aisle, but I eventually put the hurt aside.

Even though my mom lived on the other side of the world, I was determined to have a relationship with her. There were great things happening in my life and I wanted to share them with her. It started with a couple of letters to her. I also sent cards on her birthday and at Christmas. She never wrote back. Yet I kept trying.

Defiant about having my mom in my life, I called to ask her if my new husband and I could come to Australia on our honeymoon. She said yes. I was so excited and filled with hope that I could finally have the love and acceptance from my mom that I had yearned for my entire life. I think all of the years of having to be a parent to my brother, and be strong for both of us, taught me how to be persistent. I learned to go after what I wanted, no matter what it took.

My brother wasn't as lucky. He took the years of abandonment quite hard. Each time we got together, I could see the anger written all over his face. He turned to drugs. He stole. He was homeless for a while. My brother was a mess. I was absolutely heartbroken. Somehow, I felt responsible and guilty about everything that was happening to him.

While my brother struggled to understand why no one loved him or cared about what happened to him, my life went on. It was a little more than a year after I got married that my first son was born. Matthew arrived into this world at a very healthy 10 lbs., 8 oz. just before I turned 26 years old. While recovering in the hospital from a C-section, I smiled from ear to ear as I heard people in the hallway whisper, "Have you seen the Boyd baby? He's huge!" Matthew was a big baby and wore clothing sized for a three-month-old just a few weeks after he was born.

Having kids—the responsibility of rearing good, kind, ethical, responsible human beings—is the biggest job anyone can embark on.
 ~Maria Shriver

I was so incredibly excited to be a mom. Along with the delight though came sheer terror that I wouldn't be a good mom either. Almost paralyzed by fear, I made an important decision before I left the hospital with my new son. If it was going to be, it was up to me. I would do whatever it takes to be a great mom to Matthew, the kind of mother that I ached for every single day of my life. I wanted him to know, without a shadow of a doubt, that I loved him with all of my heart and would always be there for him.

As a new mom, I really wanted my mother to be a part of Matthew's life. I wanted her to be a grandmother to him, the kind you see so often in movies. In fact, I wanted it so much that my husband and I took the 24 hour plane ride each way to Australia again when Matthew was just one-year-old. The visit was nice. It didn't do anything, though, to change the relationship with my mom.

My mom finally moved back to Canada when I was 29 years old. I remember her arriving in October just a couple of weeks before my second baby was due. When my son, Brandon, was born at the end of October he arrived into this world at a healthy 9 lbs., 6 oz. with the most amazing chubby cheeks. I loved spending time with him and I was certain that just having him here would strengthen my relationship with my mom. After all, he looked so much like her.

My mother didn't have anywhere to live when she came back from Australia so I let her move in with my family. It wasn't easy.

In fact, I suspected that it may stir up old feelings about her, ones that I had buried deep inside me. It did and in a big way! After just a few weeks of being together, I completely lost it with her in the kitchen one day. I don't know what came over me. I just kept yelling at her. I guess I needed her to know how it felt to be abandoned over and over again. We didn't resolve a lot that day but I felt a little better for getting some stuff off my chest.

We didn't live together for very long. After a few months my mom found her own place and went on with her life. Thinking back now, I don't remember her sharing much about her life with me. Perhaps she was embarrassed. Maybe she just felt bad. I don't know. Although we didn't see each other regularly, I made sure to be there for her as often as she would let me. I helped her move. I did her income taxes. She came for family dinners. I took her out for lunch on Mother's Day. I bought her birthday presents. I guess I was desperate to feel my mother's love. It seems I was chasing something that just wasn't meant to be.

When I was 35 years old, my third son was born. Michael was my tiny little miracle. He brought so much joy and hope to my life. With the umbilical cord wrapped around his neck, Michael fought to be part of our family when he was born at 7 lbs., 12 oz. Seeing Michael fight so hard to be part of our lives made me stronger. It reminded me of how important it was to be the kind of mom that my children would be proud to have.

As my three sons grew up, I tried many times to have a stronger, deeper, and more meaningful relationship with my mom. I ached for her love and attention. I just wanted her to tell me how proud of me she was. I did everything I could think of to make sure she was part of our lives. I made sure she never spent a Christmas alone. I was always kind to her. I forgave her over and over again. But, nothing deeper ever really developed with my mom.

One of the most difficult things for me to accept is that my mom has never really been a grandmother to my children. A grandmother is supposed to love you, spoil you, and then send you back to your parents. She never did. In fact, whenever my mom spent time with my boys, she only seemed to succeed at making them feel bad about themselves. Before long I realized that it wasn't healthy for them to be around my mom too much so I began limiting the amount of time she spent with them. As I pulled my family away, my mom spent more time by herself.

My three sons are pretty much grown up now and they are absolutely amazing people! I could not be more proud of them. And, just like my dad did, I always made sure they knew they were loved. I taught them to believe in themselves and their dreams. I made sure they never doubted they could do absolutely anything they put their minds to. It makes me feel amazing when they thank me for being such a good mom to them. I'm not perfect by any stretch of the imagination. I do believe the decision I made to get help and work hard to feel better again made me a different kind of mom to my children.

I don't honestly know if I will ever have the kind of relationship with my mom that I've wanted all my life. I know I need to forgive her. Not for my mother but for me. I need the peace that can only come with absolute forgiveness. So forgive her I will, again.

The past does not equal the future.
~Tony Robbins

I am one of those cup-half-full kind of people. I believe in staying positive, focusing on the best in people, and being grateful for my blessings. I also stand firm in my belief that your past really does not have to define your future, and has that ever paid off for me. I am blessed beyond words.

Ruth-Anne Boyd is a digital communications and customer experience leader, passionate about helping companies deliver WOW moments to their clients and employees. Winner of 11 awards, she has been working tirelessly with companies in the financial services, insurance and healthcare sectors in both Canada and the United States for more than 20 years. A Canadian customer experience pioneer, she developed the first-ever study tour for senior leaders to share strategies that inspire everyone to say "Wow, that company is awesome". When she's not focused on the service side of the equation, Ruth-Anne is helping companies communicate clearly as one of only three plain language communications experts in Canada.

There is no illusion greater than fear.

~Lau Tzu

Amy Brasier

My Fight To Survive

Not knowing where the sun would rise was always my issue in my younger years, taking the days and time for granted.

Thriving to be successful at a ripe young age, focusing on my career and building my empire, working fifteen hours a day to make ends meet. Well, not really to make ends meet, more like trying to give my family the best of the best.

I was a 25-year-old mom of two with a university degree and over ten certificates. Friends called me a professional student because I loved to learn and better myself. Seeing my achievements on paper was proof of my accomplishments. I was always on the go. Until just after my 26th birthday. Something happened, and it wasn't just a small little cold that wiped me out and told me to slow things down. No this was worse.

One evening after teaching a course, I wasn't feeling well and went to the hospital. Not thinking much about it except that maybe it was just a bad period, maybe I had a cyst rupture, maybe... just maybe. After hours of being tested they decided to do a Dilation and Curettage (D&C). Most of you know what that is, for those of you who do not... well let's call it a dust and clean out. The doctors prepped me to clean out my uterus and ovaries.

I was used to having D & C's having been diagnosed with polycystic ovary syndrome (PCOS) at thirteen years old. This time was different. As soon as they got near my ovaries they stopped and a bunch of the medical staff ran out into the foyer of the surgical ward! Talk about a state of panic for a mother of two small children!

I lay there, still pretty high from the medications, with only one nurse in the room telling me everything would be alright. I waited and waited, my mind thinking of all the possibilities and impossibilities. Was there an alien inside of me? What could have scared them off? I could never have imagined what was to come.

The doctor walked in with a gigantic needle and a few staff. Being the optimist and trying to lighten the mood I said "Is it a boy or a girl?" I laughed, but didn't even get a smile out of them. The doctor looked at me and started explaining the process of taking a biopsy from what was a large mass on my right ovary.

My entire world flipped inside out. All the degrees, all the money I was making, none of that mattered. Because you can't bring any of it with you. No one will be at your funeral saying, "Oh my gosh she had so many certificates and she was pretty smart!"

What had I done with my time, other then keep myself busy so I didn't have to be home in my loveless marriage? What would happen to my children? I felt like I was watching a movie, that nothing was real, or that maybe it was a bad dream I just couldn't wake up from. I wanted to scream, vomit and die all at the same time. Denial, anger and sadness consumed me.

At home that evening, I had the difficult task of telling my husband at the time, that his wife and the mother of his children had cancer. He looked at me in denial and ask why I was doing this to him, as if I was not afraid myself, as if I had planned this. His reaction was pretty normal, or so they tell me, but looking at him I was so angry! All I could think about was how selfish he was acting. Did he really believe that he is the only person that is being affected by this? How could I be with such a selfish man? Why the heck is he blaming me?

This is when the terrible thoughts started running through my head... if I just fall asleep in the tub, maybe I won't have to suffer like the people I have watched suffering from chemotherapy. What if I take some extra pills tonight for pain and numb it all? My stages of grieving had begun. I knew this was selfish of me, but I didn't care. I had a right to be selfish, angry, sad and terrified.

I knew I needed to discuss with my husband decisions regarding my Last Will & Testament, ensuring that my children would be taken care of. I also had to prepare myself to tell my closest family and friends about my condition. Then having to deal with their reactions.

We sat on the couch together, my husband still like a zombie, but my mind going over and over the treatment options the doctor had given me. Stage two. I was only 26 years old, I had two babies to live for and a business to run! I was on a journey and this world wasn't done with me yet! The overwhelming decisions, the undecided options, and worse of all, what would happen after I am gone? Would I be missed? Have I done everything in my power to be a good mother? A good wife? Friend? Daughter? Sister? I knew I wasn't perfect, not even close. I had held onto a lot of anger from my childhood, but how many people don't hold onto things from the past? What I needed to do was analyze what was worth holding onto, who to make amends with and which people I needed to eliminate out of my life. My time was precious now, how I spent each moment needed to count.

As my babies arrived home from school I smiled with tears in my eyes, feeling as though the rug was being pulled out from under my feet! How do I tell my children I might not be there to see them graduate? Wrong way of thinking, I know! But we all do it, we do the whole pity party in our head and fall victim thing. Why me? Why my children? Why? Why? Why?

Then the next morning it clicked! I was up bright and early!! Oh no world! Oh no boss man!! You can't take me yet! I have big plans!! Big dreams! I got out a large corkboard and started to dream! Yup, I create long term goals and long term dreams! It was like the devil smacked me in the face with a challenge... I was ready... but I had never been so afraid in my life.

"You got this!" I confirmed to myself. "And it's okay to be afraid, but you know that." I walked the kids to school wishing everyone a good morning and complimenting the moms that stood in line. If I could make one person's day I would fulfil my obligations on this planet. Although most of the parents looked at me as if I had a second head growing out of my neck, I still smiled and continued to compliment people as my bubbly self.

I cancelled my clients for the day, poured myself a hot bath and a lovely glass of red wine, lit all the candles in my bathroom and repeated to myself "Amy you got this." I started to do some research on doctors, treatment options, healing mechanisms, natural remedies, healthy diets and other things. This was not the end, I had to make some major changes, including a totally different outlook on life in order to achieve my goals, which at this point were surviving and loving life.

That evening my dishes stayed in the sink and I didn't vacuum, for someone with OCD this was no easy feat. My little tykes were my focus. We walked to the park and played for hours and for the first time in six years I felt like a little kid again!

With the busy lives we create for ourselves, we tend to forget how precious time really is. Until you realize you may not have the time you once thought you did. So as I stood there watching my children enjoy their afternoon with me I said to myself "No! You will not leave them! You will enjoy every moment you have with them, now get your ass in gear!" I'm not going to lie. I had days where I didn't want to get out of bed and prayed for God to take me. The rush of fear was real. "How was I going to cope?" "Who was going to raise my children?"

Over the next few months I met with gynecologists, oncologists, naturopaths and homeopaths. I researched how to break this cycle, shrink this terrible mass and eliminate it. I started on different remedies, started juicing, walking in the park and down by the beach, remembering how beautiful life was meant to be.

I did two rounds of chemotherapy, and let me tell you on those days I wanted to die! Laying on the bathroom floor, staying close to the toilet and listening to my children calling my name. The feelings that would rush through my veins were overwhelming. Getting no help from my unsupportive husband, I walked my children to daycare and then vomited in the bush, pretending nothing was wrong. I had to keep smiling for my children, I didn't want them to see me suffering. That's when I decided I needed extra help... alternative medicine let's get this beat!

So I went to see spiritual healers to help break down the 7-inch mass before it spread through my body! Which was one of the hardest things to do with two little ones running around. I had to be strong, had to beat this while swimming, not floating.

Every night I lay in bed focusing on shrinking the cyst, continued my juicing, drank apple cider vinegar and laughed every chance I got. After all, my journey with this world wasn't finished. Meditation also helped me to focus daily on healing. Being a little sceptical I figured what harm could something that was supposedly going to help me with my energy do, except for maybe heal me.

It was the appointment before my operation, and to the doctors surprise, the cyst had shrunk from 7 inches down to 4 inches!!!!! I jumped up screaming with joy! In three months I had flipped the tables around and my potential for survival had become much higher. This made me want to fight harder and face my fears dead on, it would not be me that would end up dead! We all have our fears and mine were leaving this world way too early and not seeing my little ones get married! I literally looked at the world and became fearless that day! Knowing I could achieve anything with my mind!

The only real support I had at the time was my mother and father. I was in a loveless marriage and no longer had a reason to fight for him. But I did have two beautiful little faces, that would wake me up every morning with a smile, open my blinds and show me the sun. I used to tell myself the sun is shining again, your feet are on the ground so be thankful for another day.

Sure I was scared, I was terrified of death and angry at the world. How could this be happening to me? What did I do to deserve such a disease? The one thing I wasn't upset about was not being able to have any more children because I had my precious gems! Now it was time I took out my boxing gloves and continued fighting like I had in the arena all those years ago! I didn't want to wake up in the morning anymore with no will, just wanting to stay in bed and watch sappy movies and cry all day. I couldn't give up! I had a lot to live for!

That's when I decided to get my corkboard out again and see what goals I had set for myself to achieve, adding some new ones in my excitement. I placed vacation spots, camping trips and tons of cool things on the board! I decided to place it above my bed, so when I woke up I would have to face the music and motivate myself! Every day I got stronger, there are muscles appearing in my body that I hadn't seen in years. I cut all my hair off and dyed it thinking to myself "This is it girlfriend the changes begin with you!" I started having weekends away with my girls and going to the temple to meditate and feel the humbleness of the monks.

Even though I lived with positivity as much as I could, I still had FEAR. The surgery coming up was pretty serious on it's own but I was also born with a congenital heart condition, so it was even scarier for me to go under the knife.

December 13, my day for surgery was here. I was terrified and I hadn't slept the night before because all I could think about was this better work! I had prayed, tossed and turned, and slept with the kids to be near them. Talking to the doctors I made them promise me that they would make sure I woke up. I know this is something that isn't asked of doctors, because they can't promise anything, but I asked anyway.

Waking up after surgery I was pretty groggy, but I could still understand what the surgeon was saying to my husband. They had successfully removed the adhesion that was on the ovary. They were also shocked to see that the cancer had been contained to one area and so they were able to save one ovary and my uterus! I did it! I was here! Feeling an overwhelming rush of happiness, knowing that I would be able to watch my children grow, I became thankful and proud all at once. I had hit fear right back in the face and said "Fuck you cancer, I win!!!!!"

I am now 35 years old, watching my children grow, enjoying life and holding on to each precious moment. I learned to enjoy every precious day of the sun shining and to appreciate life! I decided to make myself less busy so I could be a better mother, never forgetting how short life can really be. So I quit my job and went back to school. I also spend time with the friends and family that were there to support me through my terrible scary journey.

After going through this ordeal I have decided to become a life coach. I am leaving my busy profession behind to not only love my life and the people around me, but to help others achieve this successfully also. I want to continue to give people hope in their lives, as well as show them how to achieve happiness and to always smile. I've learned to become a social butterfly again and I'm now my spunky old self that enjoys being around people and inspiring them. Not a day goes by that I don't appreciate putting my feet firmly on the ground. I am grateful for the gift of watching the sun rise and set everyday... never taking life for granted.

Amy Brasier is a mother of three; she runs retreats and workshops for empowering woman, her passions and missions in life are to help other people through life experiences and hardships, growing up in Ontario, traveling the world from a young girl and learning where she wanted to be. Obtaining different Diplomas and certificates, as a massage therapist and medical aesthetician, she then realized her calling was more into helping other people to grow!

Amy then started working with women and empowerment programs to further their future healing and growth, to become a better version of themselves. Deciding to share her story of her own battles is a part of that journey.

Courage is the power of the mind to overcome fear.
~Martin Luther King

Kimberly Carson-Richards

A Life Lived Fearlessly: The Tale of a Teen Mom

My legs slung over the examining room table. Have you ever noticed in moments of intense stress how your five senses become amplified? I could hear the buzzing of the lights above, the laughter of people passing by the door out in the hallway, the crinkle of paper underneath me as I squirmed, the sound of my heels lightly banging on the metal base of the table. While I waited for the doctor to return with the results, I considered if I should steal some tongue depressors from the jar on the counter.

In my mind were looping thoughts that rotated between completely freaking out from anxiety, and feeling completely terrified about the news I felt sure I was about to receive.

The door creaked as it finally opened, and the doctor came in. She gave me an odd look and passed me a white stick. It had a plus sign and my heart dropped into my feet.

My first thought was, "Fuck, my mom is going to literally kill me!"

I was 14 years old and I was pregnant.

I wasn't scared of what came next or of being a mom. I wasn't thinking of the long-term repercussions. In that moment, I feared the disappointment I thought my mom would feel when she found out.

I don't remember anything else the doctor said. I was in a daze. I started slowly walking home and when I was a few blocks away from my house I saw my baby's daddy standing at a bus stop.

41

We had first met in the sixth grade at the roller-skating rink. He borrowed my bad ass blue roller skates one day and we became friends. We started dating a year later when I was in grade seven.

We had recently broken up. He was waiting for the bus to go see another girl. I approached him and told him I was pregnant. Then the bus pulled up, he got on and left me standing there. I watched as the bus pulled away and I felt completely alone and afraid.

I walked the last few blocks to my house and ran to my room. I sat there and couldn't think of what to do. Then I remembered that everyday at school, I would stare at a poster for the Kids Help Phone and I knew the phone number by heart. I called and talked to a woman, who I will never know or recognize, for hours upon hours. I cried, she listened, I wailed, she consoled. She talked about the options I should consider. When we got off the phone I felt better but still terrified to tell my mom.

So, I did what I think any scared teen would do. I didn't tell my mom right away. I hid my morning sickness. I hid my overwhelming tiredness. A few weeks went by and a health nurse came looking for me at my school. She wanted to know if I had gone to my regular doctor for a check up. I knew it was time to tell my mom because the nurse was likely going to check in at my house in the next few weeks.

It was almost Easter and I was going to visit my grandma. I left my mom a letter and told her in it that I was pregnant. When she found the letter, she called my grandmother and told her to tell me everything would be okay. My mom was only thirty-one. She had been a teen mom too. I can't imagine what was going through her mind when she read that letter.

I thought the note would make it easier. Well, it didn't. When I returned ten days later, my mom and I couldn't talk about the situation without fighting. There was a lot of silence. She wanted me to put the baby up for adoption. I was dead set against it. I was stubborn and felt determined to keep the baby. I wasn't willing to listen to any rationale she had otherwise. In hindsight, I think her reaction was one any parent of a fourteen-year-old would have. But in my mind I thought she was mean and didn't understand me at all.

As my belly grew, I knew I wanted to keep my baby even more. Even though I knew the baby's father would not be able to support me. Even though I knew it would be hard, that it would change the course of my life, I still felt deep down it was the right decision to make.

After a few months my mom came around. I remember we were in the grocery store walking by the baby section and she said, "I think it will be neat to have a baby around." I knew that meant she would support any decision I made.

It was a moment of intense relief for me. I had been worried and feeling overwhelmed that I might have no choice but to put my baby up for adoption. If my mom didn't support my decision, it would be difficult for me to do it alone. The relief I felt led to intense happiness. I knew I had it in me to be a great mom. I knew my baby was going to grow up to be an amazing person.

As all of this was happening I was transitioning from elementary to high school. I was to be the class valedictorian for my grade 8 graduation. I stood all bright eyed, feeling excited in a pink polka dot dress. I gave a speech to my classmates, teachers and parents about what the future might hold for us. I was already 4 months pregnant and I was imagining how significant the changes for me were going to be. I was about to embark on a life-changing challenge for my young age. Yet I was oblivious to the enormity of the changes that were to come.

I selected a high school that had a daycare in it. The year my son was born, teen pregnancy in the city I lived in was at its highest per capita rate. I was another statistic among many. Just another teen parent, although a few years younger than most.

As I settled into grade nine, it felt difficult to care about school. I was focusing on my health because I wasn't gaining enough weight and I was feeling exhausted all the time. Plus, it was way more fun to skip class to hang out with friends. However, as my due date approached I started to realize that if I wanted to create stability in my life I needed to focus on my education. I started to consider what my plan would be when my son was born.

My mom was seventeen when I arrived into this world, and she had dropped out of high school. When my son came along she was a single parent of two kids struggling to get by. She had mostly worked in restaurants and I recognized her financial difficulties. I knew I wanted to create lifelong stability for myself and my baby. I remember my mom always told me not to repeat her mistakes. Her experiences made me realize I wanted to graduate and do it at the same time as my peers.

My baby was due in late November and I had a plan so that I would not fall behind in my studies. I would get homework for the days I missed and return as quickly as I could after he was born.

My little bundle of joy, Jonathon, arrived a week overdue in early December. I had a difficult delivery because he was so big in comparison to my tiny body. I had only gained 22 pounds and he was over eight pounds! My doctor expressed her shock at his robust birth weight. He came into the world healthy, happy and beautiful.

The night he was born, when I was alone in my room, I pulled out my unicorn diary, the type with a metal lock on the front, and carefully thought about what I envisioned for our future. I knew I wanted to be more than a statistic. I knew I didn't want to be a teen mom who spends her entire life living on social aid or working in low paying jobs. I knew if I wanted a better life, I had to get my high school diploma.

I set out three goals that night: (1) Finish high school and graduate on time, (2) Go to university to get a bachelor's degree, and (3) Surround my son with loving relationships so he always had someone to talk to when he felt like he couldn't come to me.

I wanted to set him up for success so that he could be a happy, healthy, contributing member of society when he grew up.

After he was born I only missed two weeks of school, had two weeks of winter break and was back to write midterms in January. My mom watched Jon while I was at school and I would care for him when I got home. I did my homework after he was asleep.

The following school year he was old enough to attend the daycare at the school. My morning routine became; pack him up in a snuggly, grab his baby bag and my backpack, then off we went together to take two city buses to school everyday.

As much as my mom tried to support me, I just didn't want to live with her. It was difficult to manage my relationship with her because we didn't have effective communication skills. I was struggling to get along with my younger brother. Then my mom's boyfriend moved in, whom I despised, and it added an extra layer of complexity to our situation.

I craved my independence and desired to care for my son without having to manage the relationships of living with other people. I was in grade eleven when my son and I moved out on our own.

I got a two-bedroom suite which felt like complete freedom and independence. I had a junker of a car that my mom bought me for $200, so I could drive to school everyday. By this time I worked two days a week part-time at a bank. Life felt glorious. I was sixteen and had total independence to make my own choices. I was rocking it out at school, doing well at my job and looking after my little guy.

Many people ask me if it was hard being a teen mom. I just don't remember it feeling hard. My son and I had a lot of fun together. I had a routine. It was my life and I was living it how I chose to. It is only with time and retrospect that I saw the courage I had, the responsibility I took on, and the difficult choices I had to make.

I have an intense memory of sitting in a restaurant with my mom and my son. I was feeding my son and I remember people staring at us in confusion and I'm going to guess judgment. In that moment, I made a very conscious decision. I would not allow the judgment or opinions of others to ever have any bearing in my life, unless I felt it was valid. I see now that was the moment when my deep confidence formed which has carried me through my life.

There have been times that people have said words to my face or behind my back such as "slut" or "whore." In school other girls would start rumors. But it never affected me. I wouldn't allow it. To be free from feelings of judgment at such an early age helped me immensely. Even now, at the age of 41, I still see my peers struggle with the fear of judgment. It makes me determined to help them see how it affects their decisions and outlook.

Now don't let me mislead you into thinking I was a perfect parent. I had many missteps and stumbles. I spent many weekends out dancing at the clubs and acting like a teenager. I did crazy things like stay out all night on a Friday and go to work on a Saturday without sleeping. I dated guys just like my friends were doing.

I was fortunate that I had family to help care for my son, so I had the ability to go act silly and still have fun. I had a unique dichotomy of being responsible and mature for my age, and yet getting to act like a teenage girl trying to find her way in life.

My biggest challenge, at that time, was that I disliked school so much. I often think to myself I would have dropped out if my son hadn't come along. Having him helped me stay focused on my goals.

I remember my son as being carefree. He was always laughing. He had a deep love for Batman. When he was about three years old he would run around the house in a cape, yelling "Nanananana... Batman!" As he got older he loved Beyblades and video games. We would do fun things together like go to the arcade and the beach in the summer. He was a fun dude to be with.

As planned, I finished high school and was on the honor roll. I set my sight on university. I had no idea what I wanted to be 'when I grow up.' I didn't know what I wanted to major in, I just knew I wanted a bachelor's degree on my resume when I went out into the workforce.

The summer after I graduated from high school, I met a guy that I would go on to date for five years. Our relationship was not easy, and it made university more difficult then I imagined. As much as I tried to keep up with the pressures of being a parent, working part-time, my school work and managing my romantic relationship, I started to fall apart. In my 4th year of university, I started a downward spiral into depression.

I was only able to focus on my son. I stopped opening my mail, I quit my job, I was going to class intermittently. I tried so hard to keep my shit together, but I couldn't. I stopped talking to everyone except for a few people. I was failing most of my classes.

The worst part was I didn't recognize what was happening. I didn't know I was depressed until I went to see my doctor for a check up and broke down in tears. She recommended I go on antidepressants and I flat out refused.

In an act of pure defiance against how she told me I should deal with my feelings, I willed myself out my depression. I planned a new course of action. This situation taught me a lesson; that taking steps in an action plan leaves no room for fear. You can't continue to feel stuck and afraid if you are moving forward.

I realized because of my depression and skipping so many classes, I was going to have to attend school for an extra year to get my diploma. I also realized it was time to leave my relationship for good. As my fifth and last year of university started, I moved out of my boyfriend's house.

I firmly believe all things in life happen in the exact order at exactly the right moment. Every struggle teaches a lesson.

On the first day of classes, that fall, I met a cute guy. Oh, he was so cute. We chatted before class started. Then on the second day of class I looked around the room for him, when I saw him I went and sat in front of him. I turned and asked if he had sat next to me last class and he said, "Nope."

I remember feeling intensely embarrassed that I was talking to the wrong person, but in that moment I made a choice that changed the course of my entire future. Instead of allowing the awkwardness to overwhelm me, I confidently reached my hand across to him and introduced myself. We had three classes together and I quickly found out that he was kind, patient and a great listener.

A few months later, I started dating this amazing guy that I like to say, is "the best mistake I ever made." We have been together for almost 18 years now. Regan is nonjudgmental and always calm.

He has taught me so much about what a healthy relationship is meant to be like. He quickly bonded with my son. Without fail he has been nurturing and supportive of our little blended family.

So, I have carried out all the goals I set for myself when I was fourteen. I finished high school with honors, I finished university and have a 4-year degree in Sociology.

If you recall, my last goal was about my son. To surround him with love so he could grow up to be a happy, healthy, contributing member of society. How did that turn out you wonder?

Firstly, I embraced all relationships that would support him. I reached out to his paternal grandfather. He became a wonderful source of support and encouragement for my son. As a teenager Jon spent many weekends at his grandpa's, hanging out and playing video games.

He had a relationship with the parents of my ex for many years. They have always been kind and so supportive to my son.

My in-laws embraced my son wholeheartedly and treated him beyond wonderfully. He was their first grandchild and was spoiled accordingly.

My mother was his 'go to' on weekends until he was a teenager. Without fail she would care for him when I was working, needed to do homework or just so I could go out with friends.

I had an aunt who was also a huge support. Her daughter was only one year younger than Jon, so they spent many weekends and evenings together.

With all the love around, how could he fail?

When Jon was 23 years old he decided to enter provincial politics. He was young compared to what is considered a typical candidate, although not the youngest. It took great courage on his part because he faced a lot of ageism.

Some people told him he had no chance of winning. But he had a tenacious drive and dedicated himself to the process. He knew he wanted to make a difference. He ran his grassroots campaign from our living room with the help of his girlfriend, a few close friends and family, until more volunteers came on board. It was exciting for his stepfather, nana, little sister Mikaelyn and I to see him flourish as he chased his goal.

He won the vote!

He was the third youngest member of legislature in our province elected that year. It was a moment of immense joy for me to see the beaming smile on his face as he was sworn in a few weeks later. If there is a word a million times more intense than proud that is how I felt.

Now he is engaged to his high school sweetheart Kailey, diligently dedicated to his profession and creating a life I couldn't have even imagined for him that day he was born.

My three goals, set out when I was fourteen years old, have now all been achieved.

We overestimate what we can achieve in one year and underestimate what we can do in three. I set out a 20-year goal and can tell you that it was key in helping me have the courage to show up for myself and my son every day.

What was to come next? I believe in perpetual forward motion. Creating new challenges to push myself forward. Learning new skills to expand my mind. After university, I had set my sights on all those things society tells us to strive for. Get married, buy a house, and build a career.

I spent over twenty years in business environments, progressively working my way up the corporate ladder until I landed a job I loved. For the first time I understood how different it felt when you were passionate and completely dedicated to what you were doing.

The problem was that this job I loved was a temporary position. In my mind I thought I would rock it out so hard that my boss would either leave me in the position or create something new, so I could continue doing what I loved.

But it didn't happen that way. I remember the day the boss told me I was going to get a demotion back to my old position. I was so shocked and overwhelmed. It was not how I had envisioned it happening in my mind. For the first time in my life, I felt like I had no control.

One day as my boss was talking to me about all the reasons I should just "suck it up" about how I was feeling, I heard a tiny voice. Maybe my subconscious? It said "You have a choice. You always have a choice. It's time to leave."

This thought was surprising to me because my whole life, up to that point, I had always tried to choose the most responsible decision. Even when it meant staying at a job I didn't love. I am a very logical, analytical type of person. I knew I needed to trust my intuition and that the Universe would give me what I needed next.

My courage was about to expand outside my comfort zone. I decided to start my coaching and mentorship business to help other women find their confidence. My mission is to empower women like you to create the courage to overcome your biggest critic... the voice in your head.

I have spent my life building the foundation to be a mentor and life coach without realizing it. I overcame adversity and obstacles that might have sent another person down a path of resignation. I never allowed myself to be a victim of circumstance and as a coach, I can easily help my clients find their limiting thoughts, where they allow themselves to stay stuck.

One of my clients once said I was "really good at calling her out on her shit." It makes me laugh but it truly sums up what I get to do for my clients. I am skilled at seeing the big picture and then giving new ways to think about the situations that can feel like the most difficult to solve.

I love the feeling when a client tells me they made the hard decision, or started the project that made them feel afraid, or had a difficult conversation with a loved one in a calm, loving way. I love that I can help my clients create the life they dream of and that I can be a cheerleader in their corner telling them what an amazing badass job they are doing.

This experience as an entrepreneur has been liberating. For a second time in my life, I chose the unconventional path and made a decision not well understood by others. It has been an intense period of exponential self-growth for me.

In this journey I have discovered the power of being open and vulnerable. When I share my story from a stage, I can create a connection with another person. That I inspire others is humbling and fulfilling. I LOVE speaking in front of a group of people! Feeling the rush of excitement, the slight nervousness and the payoff when people tell me they can in some way connect with my story.

Public speaking is named, by most people, as their biggest fear. My newfound love of sharing my story from a stage has inspired me to help others do the same. When a client reaches out to tell me they were able to confidently share their story in front of a group of people, I feel intense joy and excitement for them.

Making an impact on the world in any small way has been a dream since I was a child. I have finally figured out how I was meant to make my mark on the world!

Now I get to help other women create success everyday. I have come to understand success is not only about money. Success and fulfillment can come from choosing to be more present, by disallowing fear to rule your decisions, by creating more meaningful connections with those you love. What success and goals are you striving for right now?

My life has been unconventional. But each experience has shaped me into a person I am proud to be. I am a person who can say, "Fuck you fear" and move boldly forward, no matter what obstacles lay ahead.

I encourage you to choose the path less traveled. To make the less popular choice. Listen deeply to your intuition with your heart, instead of your head. May it lead you down a beautiful, courageous path where everything you ever wanted or desired will be found along the way.

"Your time is limited, so don't waste it living someone else's life. Don't be trapped by dogma - which is living with the results of other people's thinking. Don't let the noise of others' opinions drown out your own inner voice. And most important, have the courage to follow your heart and intuition."
~Steve Jobs

Kimberly Carson-Richards is a Certified Business and Personal Coach, speaker and author, who has a passion for helping women entrepreneurs increase their self-worth and their net worth.

She has appeared on numerous podcasts, written for blogs and has made special appearances at numerous women's events. In 2017 she was nominated for 2 separate women entrepreneur awards as a woman who leads, motivates and inspires. She is also the co-founder of a women's networking group called Powerful Women Unite. She lives in Edmonton, Alberta with her husband, Regan, daughter, Mikaelyn, and their fluffy dog, Tika.

Visit her website at www.forwardmomentumgroup.ca

I'm not afraid of storms, for I'm learning how to sail my ship."
~Louisa May Alcott

Shawna Flinkert

I Am Enough

I ran away from home when I was just four years old.

This was probably my first memory of what would follow me through childhood, the hormonal teenage years and right into adulthood. A memory of a scared little girl that was sure that one day, someone would tell her that they didn't need her anymore. A memory that has shaped and formed my life in so many ways and to this day still stirs the emotion that I fight day in and day out.

I honestly can't tell you how much of this is a distant memory of that little girl and how much has been created from the stories that my mom has told me.

My brother and I were outside playing in the park. A small playground that was typical of the era; a swing set, teeter totter and monkey bars. It was the height of summer, and the air was filled with the sound of children's laughter and an underlying feeling of excitement. The sound of a car approaching broke through our laughter and we both looked up in anticipation to see who was coming. It was Dad!

Dad had gone off to the hospital that day to return with our mom and our newborn baby brother. Excited to see them home and anxious to see the newest little addition to our family, my brother and I raced out to the road to meet them. The car stopped, my dad opened his door, scooped my brother up into the car and drove off, leaving me behind. You see, I wasn't as fast as my brother and my dad didn't see me.

Looking back with perspective, that little playground was right next to our house. Scooping my brother up and driving off with him while leaving me behind, was literally just pulling into the driveway. However, to that little girl that was left behind, it was a whole world away.

I ran away that day. I was only four and it was only to the neighbors. From a now adult perspective, I wouldn't even call it running away. I simply left.

I left because I wasn't needed anymore. My mom and dad had a brand-new baby and three other kids that were better than me, faster than me, smarter than me and prettier than me. They didn't need me anymore.

That feeling grew as I did and slowly developed into a fear that I would take with me for many years. A fear that would challenge every step that I took towards my dreams, my happiness, my life. A fear that I would see as I looked in the mirror; a fear that was always right there, staring back at me.

It has been said, that it is our first few years that shape who we become. We are born with curiosity. We want to touch and feel and explore. We want to love and be loved; to experience and grow. We don't ever think or even comprehend that we can't do, can't be, can't have.

We fall, we get up and try again. We are told not to touch, so we touch. We are told we can't have something and we ask again, and again. We push every limitation that is placed in our path and we plow forward without hesitation, without constraint, without fear. We are unstoppable.

Then we learn. We learn that it hurts when we fall. We learn that it hurts when we push our limitations and we fail. We learn that it hurts when we love but we aren't loved back. We learn, and what we learn shapes us, molds us and becomes us. It's like a silent disease creeping in and taking over our bodies, running through our veins and seizing our muscles, until we no longer have any control.

Running away from home is my first memory of feeling like I didn't belong. Anywhere. It is my first memory of what has become my greatest fear. Fear of not belonging, of not fitting in, and of not being accepted. Fear of not being enough.

Another memory haunts me of a time not long after that incident. A time of trauma that was buried as deep as a five-year-old girl could bury it. A memory that today is still as prominent as it was 20 years ago, 30 years ago, 40 years ago. A memory that is like a recent dream.

I can still smell the alcohol on his breath and the pungent body odor as his face got close to mine when he kissed me. I can still feel his mouth, it tasted disgusting. I can still feel the paralyzing fear that ran through me as he reached down my pants and touched me where I was not allowed to be touched. I can still hear the silent screams that filled my entire being while I just stood there in fear.

In fear of how much trouble I was going to be in! A little five-year-old girl fearful of being in trouble. Fearful that my parents were going to be mad at me. Mad at me for what? For being there, where I wasn't supposed to be? For letting a dirty old man touch me where no one was supposed to touch?

I wasn't old enough to understand that it wasn't my fault; that I was the victim. I was only old enough to understand that it was wrong and that my parents were going to be angry. I was only old enough to believe that I would no longer be loved.

I wasn't supposed to be there. I wasn't supposed to talk to strangers. I wasn't supposed to go in his house. I wasn't supposed to leave my brother alone. And I knew. I knew when I walked into his house that I was doing something I shouldn't be doing. I knew, but I did it anyway. I knew that what had happened was very bad and I knew it was my fault. I knew that I was no longer the good girl I had tried so hard to be, and now my mom and dad wouldn't want me anymore. I knew it and I feared it, and that fear became me, so I didn't tell. I still have never told. Until now.

What makes a little girl want to fit in so bad? What makes a little girl think that she isn't enough, and fear being tossed away because she isn't wanted anymore?

I didn't have a bad childhood. I was brought up in a family surrounded by siblings and loving parents; with a mother that stayed at home and was always there for us. We didn't have a lot, but we did have family. We had consistency, we had a good home and we had love. There was no abuse. My parents were strict, but they did what they knew how to do. They did their best.

So where does that fear come from? From being left behind in a mall as a small child, trapped behind the big glass doors that I was too little to open and watching my parents drive away without me, to walking away unannounced at a birthday party and rushing home because our family was moving, scared that they would move without me. Fear crept in and took a hold on me, ever so slowly.

From being bullied in school for being ugly and four-eyed, to feeling invisible in the shadow of my brother and sister, who were much more outgoing than me. Invisibility and insecurity wrapped their arms around me and invited fear in.

Fear is ingrained. Fear is taught. Fear is learned. And fear consumes. I was a very shy and reserved child. I didn't say much and really didn't have many friends until years later. I went to school every day, but I couldn't wait to get home. Home was safe, and as long as they never found out how bad I had been when I went in that man's house, home was where I belonged.

That insecure and fearful little girl grew into a teenager that rebelled in subtle ways. I was probably too fearful to rebel in great ways, so my rebelliousness came mostly in the form of self-sabotage. Partying too much just to fit in. Boys that never appreciated or deserved my attention usually got my attention and more. Skipping school and dropping from an honor roll student to barely passing my classes to quitting just a few months before graduation.

Excuses followed..."I couldn't go to university anyway, my parents wouldn't fund it." "My dad didn't support education." "I was raised that hard work was the only way you got what you wanted in life."

Every one of them were excuses. Every one of them were justification for my own self-sabotaging behaviors. Every one of them were a reason to stay safe and cover up for what I feared the most. Fear of failure, fear of change, fear of success, or just fear of oneself? Fear of not being enough!

I took that fear and protected it deep within my soul, so the outside world didn't see it. To my peers I put on a face of confidence, of strength, of stability; but in reality, I simply became a 'yes' girl. I did whatever it took to fit in and be accepted.

I went on to spend years in an emotionally abusive relationship that wiped away any self-confidence that I had gained throughout my teenage years. In this relationship I was not allowed to socialize without him. Life in our house became intolerable for days or weeks if I even suggested doing something with my girlfriends.

I learned to make excuses and opt out of invites until eventually I didn't have any close friends anymore. I made new friends, but they were always 'our' friends. If I ever seemed to spend too much time, or get too close with anyone, something would change. It was always subtle, but he would somehow make sure the relationship wouldn't thrive. If I was later than normal getting home after work or a run to the store, I was interrogated. So, I got home on time. I avoided conflict at all costs to 'make things right,' to be accepted.

You can't possibly believe this can happen if you have never been in this situation. Even having lived it, it is hard to understand how it did happen. It is like water dripping on concrete. The individual drops just bounce off but over time, with that consistent drip, it wears a hole where you never thought possible.

It was just easier at the time, and the next time, and then the time after that, to avoid conflict. Eventually it became easier to not even try. Every little excuse and every little avoidance became a small brick that contributed to the wall I was constructing around me. A wall that was built from that fear of being discarded, that fear of not being enough. A wall that by the time I realized I had even built, was too high to climb.

From other people's point of view, I had it all. Completely put together. A family, a great job, a nice house in a great neighborhood, the annual vacation; the whole package. What they didn't see were the hidden tears when I felt invisible to the world around me. The rashes that would cover my body while I pushed the stress inwards, and eventually the anxiety that controlled my sleep patterns and many of my waking hours. Cancelled coffee dates and happy hours with my girlfriends, because I couldn't bear having to pretend that my life was perfect one more time or make up a lie or excuse to avoid conflict at home.

What they didn't see was that insecure little girl still hiding within me, that insecure little girl looking back at me in the mirror, that was trying so hard to get up the courage to say, "No more!"

Then the day came. The day that I realized that even there, buried behind that protective wall, I had not been enough.

It was winter, sixteen years in, and our relationship had been going through a rough time for a while. A year or so prior I had been offered and accepted a new job, which I felt I was very fortunate to have, but had caused a lot of ripples in our 'home life'.

Not only did this career change come with some travel requirements, but our company was also primarily male dominated. Travel and company events were sore topics at home and I became fearful of telling him when a work-related trip was approaching.

It wasn't a physical fear, it was purely emotional. It was psychological. It was a fear of the following days or weeks of conflict that would follow. The fights, the silent treatments, the underlying accusations and the tears. After every single trip I was accused. Accused of not calling often enough, accused of not wanting him to come, accused of fooling around while I was away.

Everyone around me thought I was so strong and so independent... but I wasn't strong. Avoidance was easier for me, every time. I was a fraud.

In the first fourteen years of our relationship, we had never spent a night apart, not once. Everyone around me told me how odd and unhealthy that was, but to me it was just the way it was. Being away from home with my new job was like sunshine finally breaking through into a room that had been dark for a long time; you don't realize it's missing until you can see again.

I started spending time with old friends and most importantly I started spending time with myself. I began enjoying my time away and dreading each time I would be heading home. Knowing that I would be confronted with an underlying or straight out accusation and barrage of questions as to how and with who I had spent my time.

Being home became harder and harder and I found strength in my work and my ability to escape. Looking back, the best way to describe it is that I grew, and that hole in the concrete that had formed over the years was starting to crack.

That particular winter, I had been scheduled to have a hysterectomy. Hysterectomies are not that uncommon, but mine was to be a more extensive procedure due to some additional complications and would require a longer than normal recovery period. The decision itself came with hesitation and emotion, and then to top it off he accused me of wanting the procedure so that I could use it as a form of birth control with my 'extra-curricular sexual encounters' that he always accused me of having. Are you kidding me? The crack in the concrete grew bigger.

At some point around this time, he had taken a promotion that required him to work in another city, so he was only home on weekends. I had encouraged it and believed that it would take away the underlying issue of my own work-related travel.

My surgery was scheduled for a Monday in the middle of December. I would be in the hospital for five to seven days and would need assistance with daily activities upon being released. With my blessing and insistence, I had him take me to the hospital and once I was admitted, he headed off to work for the remainder of week.

Our weather was nasty that year with many snow storms and bad road conditions, so I didn't think it necessary that he brave the bad roads to see me mid-week. The weekend, followed directly by Christmas break, would come soon enough, and he would be home for a ten day period when I was released.

Surgery went well. The bad weather continued, it snowed, and it snowed. On Friday morning, five days following my surgery, my doctor released me with the assurance that I would have someone at home to stay with me. He wouldn't be home until late that evening, so I had some friends pick me up.

Later that day he called to say that he was staying over the weekend and would not be home after all. The roads were too bad, and he only had half a day of work the following week (Christmas Eve) and didn't see the point in driving home and then returning for one day. Are you kidding me? That crack in the concrete grew bigger.

I had planned to do some Christmas grocery shopping after my surgery, but I couldn't drive, so over the weekend I left him a message to have him pick up some last-minute things and I emailed him a list. When I got no response, I started to get worried. It was still the weekend, so I waited and on Monday morning, Christmas Eve, I called his direct office number and his cell phone which went to voicemail, and finally, I called his office's main switchboard. The office was closed. They had closed for the holidays on Friday! He hadn't had to work on Monday after all. He had chosen not to come home. He had lied.

I made one more call, to a mutual friend. It was reported back to me that he had been around over the weekend but hadn't been spending many nights there.

I sat frozen, exhausted from worry and recovering from my surgery, and realized what had been in plain sight for so long. All the little red flags that I should have seen suddenly became so obvious. The weekends he stayed away and the distance and change in his demeanor when he was home. His phone ringing late or in the middle of the night. His sudden disinterest in me.

My heart broke and I can't even begin to explain how low I felt. It was Christmas Eve and I felt like my whole life had just fallen apart. I felt more alone than I ever had in my entire life. I crawled into a fetal position and I waited. I waited for noon to come when I knew he would call as if everything was normal; as if he had just finished work for the day and was on his way home. After sixteen years you just know and true to form at 12:15 p.m. the phone rang.

All the years of accusations and innuendos that I was cheating. All the years of avoiding talking to that neighbor or that friend so that he wouldn't confront me with an unsubstantiated accusation. All the years of making excuses to my girlfriends. All the years of walking on eggshells and in the end he did exactly what he had accused me of doing. All the years of accusations came flooding through and that crack forming a hole in the concrete broke wide open.

Two days later I left that toxic relationship. It was the hardest thing I have ever done. There were tears, rivers of them, there was heartbreak so deep that I felt it in the pit of my stomach, and there was fear. Fear of starting over, of being alone, of never being enough for anyone.

I never told anyone what really happened throughout that relationship or how I had felt all those years, and I never showed anyone who I really was... a scared little girl wanting someone to think that she was enough.

They say that time heals all wounds and while that may not be true, time did help. As I recovered physically, I also started to recover emotionally. I dragged myself out of bed each day and spent many hours becoming acquainted with me, with what

I liked, what I wanted, who I was. I faced up to the real me and introduced her to the person I had always pretended to be.

I made a conscious decision to find the good in my circumstances rather than the worst. I came and went when I wanted to, and I neither explained nor apologized to anyone. I reached out to old friends and I made new ones.

I took it one day at a time, but I started living. I took salsa lessons and I started painting again. I traveled to places I had always wanted to go. I did everything I hadn't been allowed to do and a lot of things that I was scared to do. I even started to enjoy simply being me. It wasn't easy, in fact, it was hard, but it was so worth it.

I followed my entrepreneurial dreams and got involved in a little business that the old me wouldn't have had the confidence to carry through. The old me would have 'pretended' for the outside world but would have buried any possible success behind a pile of fear disguised as excuses.

In that little business I found something that I never expected. Away from the structure of a corporate world and the expectancies we as a society put upon us, I found a community; a place of belonging and I formed bonding friendships with other women that I met from all around the world. But even with that, it wasn't easy.

We don't just wake up one day as a different person. We are a work in progress. Fear and insecurities are ingrained in us; bad habits that are so easy to fall back into, an addiction that needs to be overcome. It is a process. A process of growth that we need to work on every single day.

My business boomed and I was eventually able to leave my job, allowing more time to follow my heart and work with other women that were struggling, just like I had at one time.

I had seen so many women, that would struggle to come out of their comfort zones, quickly run back behind that wall of security and safety as soon as things got a little scary. Or simply cave under the pressures of their lives, pressures that often they had placed there themselves. I had seen so many women give up on their dreams because it was just easier, and I wanted to help.

So, I got to work. But then something happened. Every day I would start with a new plan, but I would only get so far and then I would just stop. I would start a new project, develop a new idea or course, but I would never launch it. There was always a reason; something else important to do or a distraction. A fear disguised as an excuse.

A fear that resulted in procrastination and failure to launch, as all the old insecurities came back. I started comparing myself to other women. Women that had more experience or more success. Women that were prettier than me, thinner than me, younger than me, more vibrant than me and stronger than me.

That insecure little girl started looking back at me in the mirror again and all my fears resurfaced. Fears that I would fail them, that I would leave them trapped, that I wasn't good enough to help other women.

My fear ran deeper this time. I was no longer that little girl that could run back to the safety of home or that wall I had constructed so many years ago. I was an adult with many responsibilities and I no longer had a corporate paycheck and the security that comes along with it. I was solely dependent on this business, so busy working on it that I had stopped working on myself. I had fallen right back into the old habits, thoughts and fears. What if I wasn't good enough?

Eventually, after wasting away a year while my business declined, getting my shit together required a level of honesty that I had not been willing to face before. The realization that I, and I alone, was the only thing holding me back. I was the one making excuses. I was the one procrastinating and wasting my days away 'busy working' but never finishing anything. I was the one comparing myself to others. I was the one hiding in fear of not being good enough.

I was the one that feared the success that I knew was just around the corner. Because, with success comes change. Change in ourselves, in those we surround ourselves with, and in what we have become comfortable with. Change in how others see us and depend on us. Change takes work and forgiveness.

Forgiveness towards the people in my past that did what they knew, just like I did what I knew. Forgiveness towards that little girl that didn't feel like she was enough. That little girl that went where she wasn't supposed to that day. That little girl that got so lost in her fear and insecurity that she would have done anything to be loved and in the process had forgotten how to love herself.

Through forgiveness, I am learning that I was enough, I am enough and if someone, anyone does not see that, that is their issue, not mine.

Throughout this journey I am fortunate enough to have discovered that relationships can be healthy and supportive. My partner is my strongest supporter and is often my pillar of strength on days that I struggle. He has not only allowed me to grow but has encouraged it to the point of gently pushing me off the cliff when I don't think I am ready. And, I am often not ready.

That fear comes back and grips me by the throat more often than I would like to admit, but I don't hide it anymore. I accept it, I face it and I learn from it. I take consistent, conscious steps to rise from limitation and fear, and to embrace that I am enough. **We are all enough.**

Shawna Flinkert is an entrepreneur, business coach, and mentor to other women entrepreneurs in the online space. Having built a large team of women in her first online business, Shawna quickly realized the struggles that hold many women back from realizing their true potential, so she decided to help. Building on her previous experience as a college instructor, she founded her company Sexy Success Systems, and now empowers women to embrace their individuality and strengths, find the sexy in their systems and live life to the fullest while running their own business.

He who has overcome his fears will truly be free.

~Aristotle

Emlyn Jackson

Ugly Truth

"I want to be a woman who overcomes obstacles by tackling them in faith instead of tiptoeing around them in fear."
~Renee Swope

My will to transform from victim to survivor after divorce showed me the inner strength I never knew I had. When I look back on my decision to lift myself from the pits of my own despair, I realized I had been unsure of what to expect. Yet somehow I knew there was a more fulfilling life than the one I had in that dark, sheltered hole. Having little to no support from family and friends and lacking the money to see a professional counselor, I was alone at the start of my journey. With only my faith and blind trust in the Divine, I asked the Universe to lead me. I was shown that I was being supported and I was never alone.

Parents are my idols. My journey starts from where I remember it most. I was born and raised in a very small city named Kodiak, Alaska. I am the youngest of three children. My parents are the most hard working people I know. They have experienced so much from life's challenges.

Together they immigrated from the Phillipines to the United States and helped their family do the same. With one of them holding a high school education and the other a 3rd grade education, my parents worked very hard to move us from poverty to middle class living. They both worked full-time jobs while running a successful family-owned janitorial business.

In addition to their hard work ethics, they were very adamant about higher education being the key to a successful life.

Youngest child vs. the others. As the youngest of my family, I did not have to work as hard as my sister and brother did. In fact, I did not have to work at all. We grew apart once I hit 13 years old. Our conversations were minimal except for the times we argued. It was rare to talk about how we felt, our dreams, and our problems. Emotions were not much of a discussion topic in our family. If it didn't lead to any results, you kept it to yourself.

My parents held my older siblings to higher standards so they could help run the family janitorial business after school and on the weekends. I was spoiled by my dad, who encouraged me to do well in my studies, so he limited my social activities outside of school.

No matter what I did or didn't do, my dad was always there to take my side and protect me from sibling rivalries. My mom and I did not have a strong mother-daughter connection because she worked a lot. The most attention I received from them was either when I got in trouble (which was the worst) or when I did well in school. My parents always supported and provided for me. Their approval was everything.

I need friends. It was my norm to stay home with my nose in the books. Friendships weren't a concern of mine until I was a freshman in high school. I was always the shy girl who took pride in my school achievements for my parents. Having book smarts was not enough to influence people to want to get to know me better. I didn't know how to socialize with others.

My tactic to create friends was to participate in group discussions, agree with their ideas and validate their points. I did gain a small handful of friends who I stuck with until graduation. From them, I evolved into a meek social butterfly. It was better than not having anyone to talk to.

I was dependent on their friendship. They were my advisors in the social connection that was outside of my norm.

Over time I learned more from my high school friends about confidence and how to do my makeup and hair. But most importantly how to do what inspired me. They helped me experience a life that I had only ever read about or watched on television.

Time to leave the nest. My relationship with my parents changed when I chose to attend a college/university that was over 500 miles away. Prior to graduating high school, my parents wanted me to attend the local community college in Kodiak so I could save money. Despite their reason, I sensed their fear was really that I was not emotionally or mentally ready to leave my hometown. I remember my mom telling my dad, "Let her do what she wants to do, she will learn the hard way." As shocked as I was to hear that, I did not speak up. Instead, I took her comment as my cue to attend university with only my school smarts, regardless of my lack of real world common sense. Whether their reason was for saving money or fearful for my well-being.

I was awarded two scholarships and I was approved for student loans to finance my education. Since I had the funds for my first year of college, my parents didn't have to worry about money. My personal mission to prove that I deserved better than a small town education had kicked off to a good start! I was excited to be like all my friends who were college bound out of the city. I was damn ready for a university education and ready to learn how to become my own person. My future bachelor's degree in Human Resources Management became more than just an educational endeavor.

Not what I expected. There I was at freshman orientation, ready to conquer the world at the green age of 18 with a twinkle of aspiration in my eyes. I was alone for the first time and realized just how big the world was outside of Kodiak. I went on the usual college tour that showed me key places like the campus bus stop, cafeteria hall, classroom buildings, police station, and the wellness area. Sure, I had friends from my hometown attending the same college as me, but they weren't as close as my high school besties.

The next week after orientation, college life was in full swing! Only I struck out big time. Other than knowing my class schedule, I struggled to balance my personal life and education. Dorm life of co-mingling with strangers and dealing with diverse personalities was nerve-racking. For the first time, I was responsible for getting my own food, waking up in the morning and meeting project deadlines. Completely overwhelmed, this was a whole new norm I was unprepared for.

There were no familiar faces in any of my classes. I couldn't talk to my parents or older siblings about it. My world as I knew it had flipped. I was lonely and had zero sense of direction. I did what I could feeling alone, confused, depressed and I bottled it up.

I wasn't prepared for the major life adjustment of going from codependency to independency. My parents' fears came true. The whole ugly experience deflated the driven purpose I had to prove to my parents that I could handle college life.

Academic Probation. Yeah, you read that right! Clearly, my high school academic success did not follow me to college. My first semester as a freshman in college was an epic fail! Ugh, I bombed my first semester at college. On the bright side, there was one D among the many F's noted on my semester report card.

This was an ugly truth – my first time failing! I lost my two scholarships and was immediately placed on academic probation.

I remember when my parents asked me how well I did my first semester. My first thought was to tell them the truth, until I was overcome with shame and fear. I really didn't want to hear them saying the infamous 'I told you this would happen' speech and other words of disappointment. It was best for me to quickly end this conversation with them. So, I lied, no surprise there.

My decision to lie stemmed from my wanting to prove that as the youngest child of the family, with zero work ethic experience, I was able to stand on my own and was strong enough to break through adversity. I needed to show them that I was more than that sheltered kid who studied all the time. So I chose to protect myself from being seen as a failure by my parents. I would learn from this and quickly move forward from it.

It can only get better. With determination, I recovered very well in the second semester of my freshman year. I was off the academic probation list and I had a better outlook on how to manage myself in school. Gradually, I opened myself up to build better relationships with my teachers and connect more with others in my classes. I used the same tactic I did in high school to gain friends, but this time it was about succeeding in my classes.

I will never forget how lost I was in those first 4 months of college. When I closed my eyes, I imagined that I was randomly placed in a maze, blindfolded. I didn't know and I couldn't see where to go. I had purposely placed myself in unfamiliar territory to spite my parents.

Then, I discovered a painful reality that took me a long time to accept; I seek validation from others.

To accept that I was doing well or at least on the right track towards success, I would need to hear it from someone, especially my dad. I needed the spotlight attention and the cheering that comes with it. It meant victory for me. It was like a drug. Without it, I felt lost.

I had to force myself to let go of this need in order to embrace a life of my own without any outside influences. As fearful as it was, it was also liberating to start experiencing life on my own terms.

Then, I met him. Things were going well at school and my social life picked up. One night, my friends and I went to this new night club for patrons ages 18 plus. It was my first time hearing club music and seeing so many people having fun in one place. As I watched the colored spotlights flash and spin everywhere, one spotlight landed on him. For the purpose of this story, I will refer to him as Adam.

The spotlight shined on Adam, enhancing his white ensemble from head to toe. My jaw hit the floor and I gawked at him. I felt that I was meant to be there that night, to meet him. Luckily, we had a mutual friend who introduced us. We had one dance. From that night forward, we hung out a lot, getting to know each other better.

Adam recently served his time as an active duty member in the U.S. Army. He is also the youngest in his family, with an older brother and sister. His parents divorced when he was young, leaving his older brother to care for him as his legal guardian while he was in high school. Rapidly, I became attracted to Adam's inspiring outlook on life. So naturally I gravitated towards him when he spoke as he was like a breath of fresh air.

I felt comfortable telling him everything, from my aspirations to my fears. Everything I experienced with him was free from the judgment and worry that I had with my parents. From our conversations to having sex, we consistently created new experiences! Adam helped me with my homework and to study for exams. Whatever I needed he was there for me. He grew to be my biggest supporter and protector in everything that I did. I trusted him with everything.

At the age of 20, I was a fool in love. Adam became the greatest love I ever knew, one I had never thought could exist. I didn't expect my relationship with him to evolve into something as heavy as it did for me.

Less than 3 months into our relationship, I made plans to introduce him to my parents. I was so proud to have him in my life. Once again, I found myself reaching out to my parents for their approval and support. If my parents approved, it meant I had done well for myself.

Before that happened, I spoke to my dad about Adam, as I felt he would be more receptive than my mom. I told my dad how I met him, what I thought of him, how he cares for me, and anything else that would place Adam in a good light. If my dad was cool with the idea of Adam, he would influence my mom to be the same. The stage was set.

I forgot to mention. It worked, my parents looked forward to meeting Adam. We waited for Adam to arrive at my 2 bedroom apartment for lunch. As soon as he entered the front door it was as if an atomic bomb had gone off in the building. Aside from Adam's well dressed attire, poised posture and great smile, my parents focused more on the darker shade of his skin.

Why? Because, in the Filipino culture, any color, other than a shade of white, was considered to be less than favorable in a relationship. It was ok to date other races, but it was not considered the best choice when in a committed one.

I purposely did not mention that Adam's ethnicity is Black, Dominican.

Any good thought my parents had about Adam disappeared. They tried so hard to maintain their respectful demeanor, but they couldn't help telling me in their native language, Tagalog, how they disapproved of our relationship. Aside from him not being a White-Caucasian guy, they expressed to me that he was ok to date but not to marry.

Really, marriage? I didn't realize they could see that far into the future. I just wanted their approval. But, it wasn't going to happen.

The lunch date was very awkward for everyone. My mom barely made eye contact with Adam and my dad hardly spoke a word. Adam was squirming with sweat, I realized I should have mentioned a few key things to each of them. Adam's ethnicity to my parents and their dating preferences to Adam. Seriously, I was wrong to have believed these details wouldn't have mattered.

Ultimatum. Since we are a family that doesn't like food going to waste, we finished lunch and Adam left discouraged. Then, my parents gave me the ultimatum; if I kept dating Adam I should not expect to receive any support from them. Can I blame them? Yikes! It was harsh.

How could all this happen from not mentioning one minor detail about someone? Why couldn't they just be happy for me? I had a choice to make; be happy and keep dating Adam, or stop seeing him and not be cut off from my parents.

Blinded by anger, embarrassment, and love crushed emotions... I chose Adam.

My relationship with my parents changed. I wanted to prove to them that Adam was more than just a fling. I figured since my parents were not financially supporting my education, my decision would be easy.

Me against the world. At the age of 20, I felt like I was a rebel who knew everything. I thought my parents were against me because they rejected everything I showed them. It didn't feel that they were helping me succeed.

Along with my parents, I had friends who questioned my relationship with Adam. They gave me unsolicited advice on how different we were. I aspired to achieve my college degree. Adam had a high school diploma. I had my own apartment. Adam roomed with a friend. I had my own car. Adam did not. I had a job. Adam was former military in search of a job.

I had one close friend who dared to tell me that she thought Adam was using me. When I asked her why, she replied with, "You have everything going for you. You're beautiful and smart. Bound to achieve great things. You're taking this relationship too seriously. He's just with you because you have what he doesn't have. I don't get why you are so over the top with him." Mind you, this wasn't the first time I heard someone tell me that Adam was with me for x,y,z reasons. My thoughts were if it couldn't be proven, it was nothing but talk.

Those friends somehow drank the same water my parents did. The difference was that their judgment was based on what Adam could offer me, not the color of his skin. Like my response to my parents, I didn't give a damn because they didn't know him as well as I did.

I didn't owe any of them an explanation. But I wondered, what was it that my parents and some of my friends sensed that I didn't? Nothing led me to believe their concerns. I didn't sense any red flags with Adam.

As my relationship with Adam grew, he became my outlet to disconnect from the mess I harbored deep down inside. The mess of issues I had with my parents and my lack of sibling relationships. He boosted my morale. He helped make me shine when I felt dull inside. I was fine being vulnerable with him. I have never done that with anyone else.

I felt that those friends, aka the naysayers, were just jealous of our relationship and how happy we were. None of them could understand what I had with Adam.

After three years together, Adam asked me to marry him. I said yes without hesitation. I wanted to marry Adam because I didn't want to lose the only person who lifted my spirits and protected me when times were tough. He took the place of my parents, I looked at him now to validate my choices. Adam became the new drug that empowered my self esteem. I felt these were all the qualities I needed to build a life with someone. We planned to marry after college graduation and before I started Army basic training.

My parents didn't approve or support my decision. Aside from his ethnicity and lack of college degree, they let me know I was making the worst decision of my life. Despite their opinions, I took it with a grain of salt and pressed on to marry him. Once we were married, my parents would have to accept Adam.

In the Army now. I was in the U.S. Army and things were good for me. I felt very accomplished with my education, career, and marriage. The next step was to help Adam.

While I was in the army, I tried to do as much as I could for him. I was aware of the sacrifices Adam would have to make as a military spouse, to support me as an active duty member. Plus, he knew what it was like to serve in the army. Naturally, I thought Adam would transition well into the life and continue to support me as he had been.

I purposely volunteered to be assigned to two army base stations so that we lived closer to Adam's family and friends. The first two years were set for Fort Campbell, KY and the last two years at Fort Richardson, AK.

This didn't bring him joy. It wasn't enough. I encouraged Adam to attend a military sponsored university to obtain his bachelor's degree for free. He didn't feel ready to go back to school. Again, it wasn't enough.

I didn't know what else to do. I was lost in every way to help boost his morale. I tried to be there for him the same way he was for me in college. But he was distant.

I sensed our roles had reversed. Adam was turning into me my first semester of college, while I was assuming the role of the cheerleader and protector. I wasn't ready for that switch. We never discussed it.

I was fearful of losing him. So I told him I was ready for us to start a family. Adam wasn't ready, he had strong reservations. He felt I was too green in my military career to start a family. That I should wait a couple more years. There it was, another objection.

Someone else telling me why they think my decision is not a good idea. The answer 'no', wasn't good enough for me. I felt there was another reason and he was too scared to tell me. After many discussions and no clear answers from Adam about what was troubling him, we went ahead and started a family. We were blessed to give birth to a baby girl. Like the thought shared by many new mothers, I hoped that our baby would bring us closer. Instead, nothing changed. There was still this void that I sensed from him.

Mr. Mom and Mrs. Dad. My purpose revolved around my military career, education, family and being a wife and mother. But, not for Adam. There was no renewal for him. As a married couple, we weren't sharing successes or milestones as parents.

Since I was the active duty member, I wasn't home as much as he was with our daughter. He took care of her the most, the cooking and house duties. Adam's efforts didn't go unnoticed, but I could tell he wasn't happy. Without him saying the words, I knew he felt stripped of his masculine side. I never realized that Adam missed his Army days as he watched me report to work during the week.

When I came home, I would spend any energy I had left being with my family. I was content with what I had achieved in my life. I saw that Adam loved our daughter very much. Just as much as I noticed our love for each other was dwindling away.

I didn't know how to help Adam. I didn't know how to lift up his spirits, how to get him out of his funk. It was always the other way around.

It was a rude awakening to learn that I never allowed myself to extend compassion on a deep level to someone else. I have always been catered to, I have no experience in this area. I felt helpless. The only thing I could do was listen to Adam vent about how unhappy he was. His energetic spark was gone. I thought, every married couple in the military goes through this... we will be fine.

Tragedy strikes. I caught Adam cheating with women from an online chat room. Allegedly, he cheated on me before and while we were married. Everything that I made Adam out to be was a facade. Before the end of my four years in the U.S. Army, I was medically discharged in June 2004.

Upset with Adam, as a rebuttal, I had an affair while we were married. Months later, my father passed away. A year later I separated from Adam. My daughter and I moved in with my mom. After 10 years of bickering back and forth during our separation, our divorce was finalized.

After divorce. I thought after I signed on the dotted line of the divorce decree that I would feel happier, fearless, and regret free. Nope! Instead, I was still fueled with betrayal and rage towards my now ex-husband Adam. I gave my all to him, shared everything I had. He went from treating me like a princess, to being a shady bastard! I didn't know how I deserved him changing from being the best person in my life to the worst.

While my mom shared her 'I told you so, but you didn't listen' comments, I realized she was right. I didn't listen. If my parents had elaborated more on the word 'no', to further explain why it wasn't a good idea to marry him, then perhaps I would be in a better place. I wouldn't be a divorced, single mom.

When I didn't have my parents during college, I needed Adam to fill their place, which he did. Once I received my bachelor's degree, there was nothing left for Adam to cheer me through. When I was in the military, we gradually grew apart.

I was back to being alone, with no clarity and fearful to trust another person. Despite that, I achieved everything I was supposed to, a family, independence, career and social acceptance. I realized that it is possible to have everything stripped away from you. The life I had built crumbled like a tower built on sand.

Hard Lesson. When I look back on my life, from the time I was hell bent on attending a university, to being with Adam that ended in divorce, I recognized that I rebelled against my parents. And anyone who had something to say about my relationship with Adam.

I considered their advice as judgement towards my actions. Blindly, I was motivated to prove them wrong, despite the con-sequences of my actions. I acted out of immaturity and spite. In addition to being afraid to journey alone into the unknown, I still needed someone to guide me and validate my actions.

Consequently, those who I rebelled against tried to protect me from making poor decisions. I was emotionally triggered out of fear to run from one protector to another, until I was strong enough to stand on my own. When I finally did, I couldn't return the favor.

Life is all about choices. I could have chosen to remove the blindfold while in the maze, or I could have Adam guide me through it. I could have stood up for myself more as a springboard to grow and flourish on my own. Heck, I could have listened to my parents and stayed in my hometown after high school.

Today, instead of being ashamed of my troubles and continuing to act on my fear based thoughts, I appreciate the hard times I went through. It took me years to finally get out of my head and reflect on my life. Through a clearer, better perspective and accepting responsibility, I can see things in a much more positive light.

I may portray myself to be this awesome, badass single mom, but we are alike. I have struggles with letting go of the past and sharing my experiences into the light. It's a painful reality to share an ugly truth about myself, that I traveled a long road of codependency and grief. Although, I am highly thankful to let go and let faith guide me to share my past, that I named an ugly truth. In exchange, it has gifted me the freedom and purpose to design a life I choose to live. As I stand on my own stronger than my spiteful and younger self, I grow happier, fearless and regret free each day.

Emlyn Jackson, is the owner of Be O'Sy Spiritual. Specializing in Intuitive Mindset Coaching. She is on a mission to help people thrive through her mentorship. She is also a Human Resources Professional and Disabled Army Veteran.

She holds a Bachelor Degree in Human Resources and a Master Degree in International Business.

Emlyn is a positive change ambassador who strives to impart people with the tools, guidance, and inspiration they need to pave the way to lasting personal and professional prosperity.

Emlyn is a mom to her beautiful daughter. To relax, she enjoys meditating to piano music frequencies and painting abstract art.

I learned that courage was not the absence of fear, but the tri-umph over it. The brave man is not he who does not feel afraid, but he who conquers that fear.

~Nelson Mandela

Carmela Lamanna

Growing Stronger Through Fears

Thinking back on my childhood is both painful and fearful. I was the pawn of their jokes and they loved to scare me on purpose. The youngest of five children, with many years separating me from my siblings had its challenges, and still does to this day. Many times I have been misunderstood, criticized and made fun of, mostly because of their jealousy of me. My sister and brothers thought that I was daddy's little girl and spoiled, because I was the baby of the family. Everyone thought that I got whatever I wanted from my parents. This was untrue, but this was how they viewed it, and so for them, it was the truth. For me, the fact was that I did not fit in, did not belong, everything was a fight and a constant struggle.

My siblings constantly felt the need to put me down, I couldn't do anything right, I was always in their way and I never helped with the chores. They did not like me at all, at least this is how I felt at the time. What made things worse was that they were forced to take care of me when my parents were not around. We lived on a farm far from town and once a week, usually on Fridays, my parents would go into town to gather food and other supplies. They would leave us kids at home to take care of the chores that needed to be done. I was always trying to hang around my older siblings but always ended up getting in trouble with them.

These weekly trips my parents took sometimes meant my dad would visit with his friends and play cards at the local bar. This could turn into late nights and sometimes the whole weekend. They would not play for money, but supposedly for fun. They would all get so drunk that they would end up fighting with each other and not come home until the next day. We would all pray that my dad would come home with my mom that same day so we would all be on edge, watching for them.

It was like watching a suspenseful movie, we didn't know how it was going to turn out at the end. And when we would see my mom, coming home alone, we would all be in a state of alert. For me it was a state of fear, because I knew what this usually meant. The calm before the storm.

My dad was an amazing man, caring, funny, loving and hard working, but it was like living with Dr. Jekyll and Mr. Hyde. Once he got into the alcohol he would become a totally different man; one who was mean, terrifying to be around, scary to talk to and violent. This man would hit us and throw anything he could find within his reach at anyone who would even dare look at him. When this man came home we would go into hiding, at least until he fell asleep. Still, we had to be very quiet, because if we made noise and woke him up, we would all get the beating of our life.

There were a couple of incidents when I had to flee just so my mom would not get beaten up. One of these times was when I was very little, I remember this like it was a dream. My brother had gone to town to visit with friends and my mom and I were at home. My dad had gone to play cards at the house of a friend of his and would be home by dinner time. While my mom was making dinner, he walked through the door and I got the shivers when I saw him. His eyes had a glazed look, with almost no light in them. He went over to see what was for dinner and he just snapped. Apparently he didn't want pasta that night. He began to push my mom and as he turned to slap her, she fell backwards! He then proceeded to grab a hatchet that was nearby and raising it with his arm in the air he started yelling, "I am going to cut your throat!"

I was so terrified that I ran out the door with no coat, only boots and a sweater, it was the middle of winter. I had to get to town, even though it was an hour away and dark outside. I had to find my brother, to tell him to come home and help my mother. I got to town in what seemed to be no time at all, but I was unable to find my brother. I had no choice but to walk back home in the middle of the night. But I didn't dare go home, so I decided that for my mother's sake and mine, it would be better if I didn't go inside that night. So I slept under a broken down shed nearby. There was snow on the ground, but I managed to find a small spot that was clear of snow. The adrenalin had taken over with my fears but this was better than facing my father.

I went home the next morning, when I knew my brother would be home, thinking in my mind I would be safer. But as I was hiding behind my brother, my dad still gave me a couple of slaps and kicks, hitting me in any way he could reach me. This for me was still easier then witnessing what had happened the night before while he was drunk.

I lived in constant fear. This was also true at school, where I was constantly bullied. Although the bullying was hard, the fact that I was so used to being put down by everyone and witnessing all the abuse at home, it felt like I was not in my own body most of the time. It seemed like a dream; my body was there but my soul was gone.

At this point I was used to being the punching bag. I learned to shut down every time someone would say or do something to me. I became a shell. All the fear had stripped down my joy of living, but I was being given the gift of strength at the same time.

I was going through the motions of living with only the feeling of fear. I was even afraid of being happy, for the fear of stirring up something in my dad. In fact, we all lived in fear of saying or doing something inappropriate, or disrespectful, especially when we were out. All he had to do was look at us, and we knew exactly what was waiting for us when we got home.

I never felt like I belonged or fitted in. I wasn't pretty enough, smart enough or worth respecting. This left me feeling empty, lonely and fearful to speak up. I was just not good enough.

My only saving grace were the animals that we had on the farm. I felt close to them, could say what was on my mind and I would even cry to them. I shared my feelings of loneliness, fear and they never judged me. I could tell them anything and they showed me compassion by loving me back. I would also pray a lot to Jesus, he was my savior. I felt as if I was talking to a friend, without being made fun of for how I talked, or when I mispronounced a word. Even today this is a sore spot.

Then one day something happened that would change my life forever. I was nine years old, my mom had just warmed up some milk to add to the bowl of bread that was our usual breakfast. She sat down across from me as I started to eat. I didn't notice that she was slouched down, sliding off the chair. My dad walked in and looked at her with concern, I remember how he gently lifted her head and said to her, "Hey what the fuck, you look dead!" Then he lifted her up and asked her to walk. The last words I heard her speak were, "I have no strength, I can't do it." At this point I felt my dad panic as he looked at me and told me to run to town and get my brother and the car. We needed to take her to the hospital. I had never seen this side of my father before, always a strong man, he was now scared and panicking.

I am not sure what emotion was the strongest that day, the fear or the sadness and confusion. I'm not even sure to this day. I remember I did not run but flew to town as fast as I could. What normally would have taken an hour to walk to town one way, took me only an hour going there and back. I didn't know what to make of it. Once again I must have been numb, because I don't remember anything after that. I swear I was carried by an angel that day.

I believe that angel must have been sheltering me from the pain and the fear, because I was so numb. I was going through the motions but not feeling anything. This was the way I was dealing with all the fear in my life at this time.

My mom lived about three months after that incident. She had suffered a brain aneurysm. She was left unable to speak and unable to leave the bed. Although she could understand, because tears would flow down her cheeks when we would speak to her. She passed peacefully.

I was not allowed to say goodbye to her. My dad thought that I was too young to understand and believed it was best to shield me from this situation. I carried around so much anger and fear for many years after. The anger of her leaving me so young and the fear of not having my mom to console and guide me, to protect me from life's events.

Skipping ahead a few years I was now married with children of my own. That's when all of this emotional baggage came to surface. I had no mother I could call and count on for emotional support and guidance. I wasn't sure if I was doing a good job as a mother, wondering if I was making the right decisions. I finally understood why my mother would endure the abuse from my father; she was thinking of us and how to shelter us from the abuse. She would often throw herself in front of us to protect us. She was showing us her strength as a person and how that strength could overcome fear.

I never understood this until I had my own children. My husband didn't understand some of my outbursts. I was filled with anger and fear, I couldn't expect him to understand, but he eventually did.

Growing up and seeing how my dad would treat my mother, I vowed to never let anyone do that to me. I made myself a promise to never be in an abusive relationship.

I am so happy to say that my husband is my rock! He has taught me to work through some difficult times, to be stronger than I could ever imagine, to say F*ck Fear and do it anyway. I learnt to believe in myself and to stand up for myself. And not to worry about what other people thought of me.

This new way of thinking took awhile. I had the people pleaser syndrome. Always fearful of what people thought of me, from how I dressed, to how I spoke, to what I did. I usually didn't say anything to anyone if they hurt me or disrespected me. I would cry and vent to my husband about it and then he would push me to stand up for myself. I lived in a bubble of make believe. Outside I looked happy and confident but inside I was self-sabotaging and self-loathing. Fearful of speaking up, afraid of saying the wrong thing, to not be liked. I was always worried that they might be mad at me or not speak to me anymore. Eventually I began to listen to my husband and to stand up for myself. This was not easy to do.

I slowly started to be more assertive and less fearful of what others thought of me. And so began my healing journey of meditation and accepting who I am.

Meditation for me has been an eye opener for many different reasons in my life. It has allowed me to heal the pain from the loss of my mom and to forgive my dad. Most of all it has allowed me to blossom and accept who I really am. My heart will always ache because I lost her, but I am no longer angry at her for leaving me at such young age. I am not afraid to speak up for myself anymore.

What others think of me is no longer my business. Fear has made me stronger, I truly believe that. Fear has taught me to push through anything. The challenges keep coming, but my strength continues to grow.

I never thought I could do public speaking, especially because growing up I was made fun of for my speech impediment. I remember the first time I decided to speak in front of strangers. My heart was beating out of my chest, I was sweating like crazy and the ringing in my ears was almost deafening. I had been asked by my meditation teacher to stand in front of our congregation and give spiritual messages. I remember feeling so scared that I almost passed out, my mouth dry and the room spinning. But I had promised her that I would give a couple of messages from spirit and I couldn't disappoint her.

When the time came for me to stand up, my legs felt weak and shaky and my underarms were sweating. But I stood up and I began to speak. To my amazement words started coming out and guess what??? I was right on with whatever messages I was giving to people! Wow! I was so shocked, but most important of all... I did it!!!! I had pushed through the fear and it didn't kill me.

This is what I have learned through the years of my living with fear. Fears are there to guide us, to help us grow and succeed no matter what. For me fear pushed me past my boundaries, it has taught me that I am stronger than it is! Even when the fear was very strong, almost paralyzing, the force that was pushing me past it was stronger. I would not be this strong if I hadn't learned to fight back fear.

Obviously, if the fear was from danger then you should not push past it. You have to have responsibility and common sense. Be aware of the fear but also be aware of the situation where the fear is involved. Don't place yourself in a dangerous situation just so you can prove a point to yourself or others that you are not afraid.

Fear has its purpose and having lived with fear all my life it has now become my friend. My wish is that my two daughters and my grandchildren learn to push through their fears. With all the many lessons along the way and all the ups and downs.

I am proud to still be learning, still pushing past my fears. The ones where my mind is saying one thing, but my heart is saying another. I believe sometimes we misread our feelings, perhaps we mistaken adrenalin for fear? Or excitement for fear? I am at a place in my life now where I know when to take a deep breath and ask myself 'what if'. What if this is not real? What if I will regret not doing this or speaking up about it? What is the worst thing that can came out of this fear? I don't want to regret not doing something just because it scares me. Like deciding to write this story. I never want to regret not doing something that could help me let go of some of my pain because of the fear of what others think. So I said F*ck Fear! And did it anyway!

Fear has always been my friend, I just didn't know it. It has looked out for, guided and warned me. I have discovered that fear is misunderstood. It is that little warning voice in your head that keeps you alert, like a good close friend who will always look out for you. Fear is not real, danger is real. Become aware of the different feelings your body is sending you and when that little voice speaks up to try and hold you back, well you know what you need to say to it, F**ck You Fear! I am doing it because I am worth it.

Are we born with fear? Or do we learn to be afraid? I have always asked myself these questions and this is what I think, perhaps a little of both. If you believe in reincarnation, I would say fear is something that is built in our DNA and we bring it back with us, lifetime after lifetime. With each new life we add another layer of fear to our old ones and to undo that fear we have to slowly peel back those layers just like an onion. Slowly, one layer at the time. Some layers may make you cry more than others but by peeling back those layers you can tell it to F*CK IT! Pushing through it to heal ourselves.

Everyone has some fears, the trick is not to let it take over your life, or stop you from doing something that you truly love. Learn how to become friends with your fear, how to tell it to F*CK OFF! Do what scares you, it will be the best reward.

Reach deep within and find your strength to fight back the fears that are trying to stop you from living a peaceful healthy life. The life that you were meant to live. Find that one little light that is in your heart to help you believe in yourself again. Stand strong and proud for who you are and what your truth is. Finding your voice is finding your strength. It is never too late to take back your life from your fears. Don't let fear win. Live your life with no regrets.

Recognizing her ability as a medium a born Empath and Energy Healer, **Carmela Lamanna** drew on her lineage to cultivate and refine her skills. Doing so has allowed her to blossom and embrace her lifelong path as a Spiritual Healer and Teacher. Connecting with the spirit world has become a cherished ability and one she embraces. Receiving knowledge from her ancestors, Carmela is able to guide you to be your best self through inspirational speaking.
Rising the spirit within.
www.powerofrisingspirit.com

Courage is resistance to fear, mastery of fear,
not absence of fear.

~Mark Twain

Michele Anne Lopaschuk

Finding the Magnificent Michele

It took years and years of abuse and many sleepless nights to finally realize I matter. Once I made the decision to stop making choices based on my fears, I was able to see past the pain and hurt. It hasn't been an easy journey by far, but having the courage to take charge of MY life has given me meaning and purpose. Speaking up for myself, doing what I love to do, has given me hope and has changed my life significantly. Today I am a passionate and empowered woman.

At the young age of six, I was told that I was adopted when I was a six month old baby. I was raised in a very small town in Alberta and was often reminded by the kids at school that those were not my 'real' parents. I didn't really understand what they meant, but all I know is that it left me with deep scars, and a feeling of emptiness. I had no identity and so many unanswered questions. Why didn't my mother want me? What was wrong with me? Why did she give me up and who was my father?

I felt abandoned and hurt by the person who gave birth to me. I hated this woman, my so called biological mother, with a passion because she left me without knowing who would adopt me. It turns out that my adopted parents were verbally, emotionally and at times physically abusive. I felt unloved by 'parents' that I thought were supposed to love and take care of me. I was afraid of my parents, stepsister and certain family members.

I definitely wasn't a happy person, as I wanted to run away by the time I was 14 years old. It seemed so simple, I was desperate to find a way out and feel loved. I didn't feel wanted and just needed to find a way to leave home, so the best thing for me was to get married.

At age 16 I married a man that was five years older than me. What the hell did I know about love or marriage? How was I to know that I had put myself in yet another abusive situation. I was 16 and thought this was normal, not realizing that it wasn't right.

Exactly nine months later we had a child. Things really didn't change much, the abuse continued. I wasn't happy being with this person, but had to stay because my mother said I had to, I was married. After having baby number two, he made the decision to move to Ontario for work and as a good wife, I followed.

Our relationship was nonexistent and things didn't change. The abuse continued. I desperately wanted to move back to a familiar home but my mother disagreed and kept reminding me that he was my husband, I had to stay for better or worse. I felt stuck and alone in a city where I didn't want to live with a man I didn't want to be with. We eventually separated.

I was working at a hair salon and the owner appeared to be sympathetic and who I thought had my best interests at heart. He seemed to care and actually love me but I was sadly mistaken. My ex-husband was frightening to be with, but this one was a nightmare. Only after I got pregnant did his true colors appear. As a single mom with two kids, pregnant with my third, I was feeling very vulnerable, alone and extremely unhappy.

Twenty years ago when domestic abuse was called in, and there were no signs of injury reported, the perpetrator was not charged. That was the beginning of the next twelve, unpredictable, miserable years of living in fear. I had my third child, his child, feeling isolated, intimidated and worthless.

Every time I attempted to protect myself, things would get worse and I continued to feel stripped of who I was. He would promise over and over again that he wouldn't be like that. I desperately wanted to believe him but that was just a delusion. I felt like I was nothing, unloved and distressed, but yet thought it was okay to live the way I was.

By the time I was 25 I had five kids under the age of nine years old. I was living in a distorted reality, and couldn't understand what I did to deserve the unfortunate events that continued to take over my life. This life was taking a toll on my well-being, always feeling exhausted, unworthy, broken down, unloved and unable to trust anyone. Living in chaos was wearing me down. I just wanted to give up. I hated my life.

The feeling of being isolated and constantly worrying left me no other choice but to call my father. When I called him and explained my situation he came to the rescue and helped me move back to Alberta with the kids. What happened next was not on my radar.

Asking my parents for help was one of the biggest mistakes I made. They took total control over the three younger kids. My babies were taken and placed in foster care with the intent to be given up for adoption. This was the moment I felt my heart and soul being ripped out of my already broken body. I was devastated and began to drink heavily, didn't care about anything anymore and lost all interest in life. Who could I trust now? Hell no one.

The father of the three children that were placed in a foster home found out what had happened with his kids and came back to me. He sweet talked me into believing that everything would be ok if I returned to Ontario with him, and I actually believed him. I wanted my kids back so bad and didn't want to lose the other two. Fear took over. I was so scared after what had happened, so I went back to Ontario.

I'm now back in an unfamiliar place, living in a cheap motel with the two kids, no money and very little food. After a long battle we managed to get the other three boys back. I was so happy, I was reunited with all five of my children once again, but unfortunately that feeling was short lived. It didn't take long for the abuse to start again.

With no one to trust, I stayed in this destructive relationship in fear of losing my kids once again. My heart ached knowing that the kids were witnessing the physical and verbal abuse that I was subjected to. I felt I could protect my children. As long as he only abused me everything would be ok.

Within a ten year span I moved around with the five kids at least fifteen times, so that school teachers wouldn't catch on to the abuse I was enduring, or the disgusting unfit living conditions. I was ashamed but just couldn't cope any longer hoping someone would find me and take me away from all this bullshit. I just wanted to curl up and die.

However, things took a turn for the worse, my mind and body just gave up. Depression hit me hard. My physical body was there but my mind and emotions were absent. No, actually I was already dead. I slept all the time, I just didn't give a fuck. What kind of mother was I? There were times my eldest child would have to cook, clean and take care of his siblings. The place was a chaotic mess, the dishes were never done, floors were sticky and dirty, never washed or vacuumed. It was a repulsive environment for anyone to live in, especially innocent children.

I knew this wasn't the way to live and felt it was better if I wasn't around, sadly this lead me to attempt suicide a few times. I hated myself so much and felt like I had nowhere to turn. I was always paranoid, afraid, suffering with anxiety attacks and from debilitating headaches.

My paranoia became more evident as the days and months went by. I was trapped, nowhere to go and no one I could trust. Every night I knew the doors were locked and felt a sense of security in my small but messy room.

There were many nights while I slept that I would sense and feel something near my face, my heart would begin to race and my breaths increase. When I awoke I would see this male figure (the kids' father), his face in mine, asking me what I was doing. This man did whatever he wanted to me and I allowed it because I had no more strength. I hid the pain for so long, the pain of being constantly abused by someone who I thought loved me. I cried many nights from the pain of hurting, abandonment, not being loved, not trusting people and always being afraid of what to do or say.

The feeling of loneliness and the lack of confidence destroyed every ounce of my being. No matter what I did, nothing was good enough. Shit, even my kids didn't listen to me. My life was a mess, I was spiraling out of control with no guidance or hope. All I remember doing at this point was asking the universe for help. I wanted help, I wanted out, I gravely needed things to change or I would seriously end up in a grave. I couldn't take it anymore, all I did was hope that things would get better for us.

I'd had enough of the abuse and things started to happen after I met a woman in her 70's. She heard my story and graciously took me under her wing. She was like the grandmother I had always wished I had. She saw what was happening to me, but she believed in me and gave me the strength to leave the situation.

This is the moment that changed my way of thinking and feeling. The first time I learned about really asking for what you want and receiving it, but I didn't realize the profound affect.

Fighting seemed to be the only way that the father of my children communicated. He was a controlling, manipulative narcissist. The police were dispatched and arrived at the rental property I lived in because a domestic dispute was reported. Children's Aid was involved and because of this I vowed that this would be the last time this man would be part of my life.

My eldest child had attempted suicide a few times. This spun me into a web that brought feelings of guilt, blame and unworthiness. I blamed myself for what was happening. The last attempt landed him in the hospital. Eventually he moved in with a nurse that became his foster mother.

My second born son went to live with his father. I now only had my three younger children. I felt like my soul was not just ripped out of me again but crushed. All I could hear in my head were the words my adopted mother had said to me over and over again when I was a teenager; "you won't amount to anything and you are no good for nothing" ha, how ironic. I definitely felt like a horrible mother and worth nothing.

The father wanted visitation rights with the children. I fought, but the courts granted him supervised visits. What a disaster, those were my kids! The kids and I had to travel by bus and subway for one and half hours, one way. When we arrived there were always issues. I decided that I needed to take courses to increase my chances of getting a decent job, maybe working in an office. It wasn't easy but finally, I was successful and got my first office job.

That job was brief as I had nothing but issues with the kids. Constantly being called away, and having to take time off work because the kids were fighting all the time. The babysitter couldn't handle them and eventually quit. My kids learned behaviors that mimicked that of their father and I could no longer control them. A difficult decision had to be made, either I voluntarily gave my kids to Children's Aid or they would take them from me. This was one of the hardest things I ever had to do but for the good of the children I voluntarily gave the three boys aged 6, 8, and 10 to foster care. It felt like my whole world crumbled again.

I began to drink and party, I was out of control. Hostility set in. I was angry with myself, angry with the father of my children, angry with my adopted parents and I despised all men. Blaming others was easier and I wasn't ready to take responsibility for my own actions. My life was a fucking mess and I was doing things out of resentment. It takes a lot of energy to stay angry and I wanted to change for the better.

I was alone and this was when I started on my journey. It was time to invest in myself by healing my deep emotional and mental scars. It was a long, difficul, process of finding out who I was, learning to deal with where I was and where I wanted to go.

I still remember my first group therapy experience. That day I learned I wasn't alone.

Listening to other women talk about their experiences made me understand that not only was I not alone, but we shared relatable stories. Talk about an 'aha moment.' It was a crucial time of awakening for me.

Eventually, I started working in the corporate world, in an office processing utility bills. I was able to start visiting with my kids while still in foster care. It was extremely difficult and heart-wrenching, for both the kids and myself. I often asked myself if this was worth it, visiting my kids was like reopening a wound that hurt like hell. But I was longing to have my children in my life, so I was willing to feel the pain. I continued taking various courses to better myself, I needed to be a better version of me and be able to put all the broken pieces back together again.

What was I doing wrong? I continually gravitated towards abusive men over the next 20 years. I didn't see it, I just kept doing it. Coincidently, I married a man five short months after the passing of my father, we were married for three painful years.

Two years before I left this abusive marriage I made the decision not to take his shit anymore. I've been taking all forms of abuse my entire life and came to the conclusion that life is way too short. I often questioned myself, why me, why do I continue to take the brunt of the abuse?

One day it became very clear to me, I was afraid and just wanted to feel loved. This relationship had so many red flags. Why didn't I see them? He was very angry, controlling and demanding. He refused to change and I realized that I could not change this man. That the only person I could change was myself.

There were many times, perhaps even daily, during this marriage when I drank to the point where I could barely walk. I stumbled, had many falls and would just pass out. I often felt like shit the next day but continued to do it. Why not? It was easy and helped me forget the pain I was feeling because I was numb. I started talking to myself looking for answers.

I was suppressing my feelings because I was afraid to talk to my husband. I knew I wasn't happy, but was afraid to confront an abusive person. It was easier just to stay quiet and live in turmoil. When it is difficult to communicate with someone and they are always giving you resistance you know you have to get the hell out. I knew it wasn't going to get me anywhere.

The lessons I learned from this experience were that in order for a relationship to be harmonious there has to be mutual respect, trust, love, passion, support, communication, boundaries, empathy and compassion.

It took 23 years of investing in myself to realize that this is an ongoing investment. Loving and believing in myself fuels the power within me to do anything I put my mind to. I deserve to be happy and to have whatever I want and if I don't I just move on. I am the creator of my own life and destiny, I choose how I want to live. I am empowered to live my life helping others being inspired and motivated to achieve their goals. I believe, I have faith and am grateful for everything that I have and for things to come. I know I can't do anything when things are out of my control.

Since Sept 2017, I am proud to say that I continue to be sober. It was one of the best decisions I made. I have had several personal challenges, but can honestly say I haven't felt the need or desire to reach for alcohol. I know now that I am a strong woman, I have the courage to conquer any situation that presents itself. I have an amazing network of people in my life who truly love, care and support me. I feel unbelievably grateful for who I am today. I am worthy and I am beautiful.

Most recently, I made a decision to leave a nine year career as a Facility Manager to be an entrepreneur. I often thought about quitting my job and over the last three years, I'd had enough. Trading time for money and being bullied by female leaders in the industry. The position I held was extremely stressful and required me to be on call 24/7 to manage 90 buildings. The accumulated daily stressors caught up to me and my health was affected. That was the final straw.

The health scare taught me that life is too precious. If I wanted a better life for myself I needed to do what I love to do.

I've always said that once I was in a better place my mission in life was to help others. Inspiring them and helping them realize their full potential inspired me to be a stronger empowered woman.

Yes, it was a huge risk and not a day goes by that someone questions my sanity. The question that is constantly asked is "Are you sure you want to quit a secure, high paying job with benefits?" Funny enough I didn't give it a second thought, it just felt like the right thing to do at the right time. I immediately felt the weight of the world lifted off my shoulders.

This is by no means an easy road that I have chosen, but regardless of the limited resources, I am not afraid anymore. I am willing to work hard and achieve an abundance of success. I have faith and believe that I will attain financial freedom as I reach my goals. I know by keeping a positive attitude good things will come to me and those that I love. A valuable lesson learned, living in fear is not living at all and it was limiting my potential as a magnificent strong woman.

I learned that by loving myself I can take charge of who I am and make decisions for me. I am no longer fearful of a boss, a relationship, a child, a person or any challenge thrown at me. I am not afraid to speak my mind nor am I afraid of speaking up for what I believe in. The power of loving oneself is so empowering that everyone should be given the opportunity to experience bliss.

Being aligned with the Universe brings a feeling of unconditional love for myself and others. I do what makes me happy and I no longer accept anything less that what I deserve. I am grateful for who I am today, appreciate the people who love, support and encourage me, and I will always remember where I came from.

Letting go of things or people that no longer serve me well has given me the permission to let go of the guilt and the feeling of being afraid. It's my life and I have the power to write my story, knowing that by doing so I will live the life I so desire.

The Universe moves everything to make way for my true purpose in life, of being true to myself, helping others and most of all loving myself for eternity.

Never give up, remember you are not alone and you are Magnificent!! LOVE and LIGHT.

Michele Anne Lopaschuk, is a dynamic Entrepreneur sharing healthy products in the wellness industry. She loves to help others achieve a healthier lifestyle. She was a former Facility Manager with a large portfolio of buildings. She started her career in the Corporate Real Estate industry in 1999, where she remained for 19 years. While still working in the business sector she went on to become a Life Skills Coach and further pursed her education by becoming an Energy Healer.
She received the Outstanding Volunteer Achievement award for the Women's Centre of York Region in 2015 by the Government of Canada.

I have learned over the years that when one's mind is made up, this diminishes fear; knowing what must be done does away with fear.

~Rosa Parks

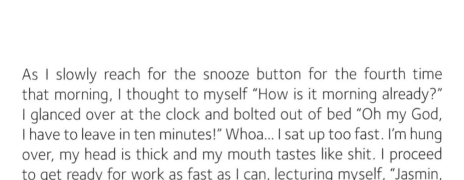

Jasmin MacKinnon

Damaged Goods

As I slowly reach for the snooze button for the fourth time that morning, I thought to myself "How is it morning already?" I glanced over at the clock and bolted out of bed "Oh my God, I have to leave in ten minutes!" Whoa... I sat up too fast. I'm hung over, my head is thick and my mouth tastes like shit. I proceed to get ready for work as fast as I can, lecturing myself, "Jasmin, when will you learn? Why do you stay up so late? Why did you drink so much on a work night again?"

I barely remember getting home. I was working two jobs, one full-time and one part-time. It wasn't uncommon to go for drinks with the staff after our shift. This particular night I had a good buzz when I left the pub. Regrettably, I occasionally drove after drinking a few. I know, not cool. The highway was pretty quiet at 3:00 a.m. I rocked out to some Alanis Morissette while cruising home, except I fell asleep... or did I pass out? All I remember is coming to and thinking "Oh my God! I'm still driving!" or more like drifting. The car was crossing lanes and going less than 80 km/hr on a 120 km/hr highway. OH. MY. GOD. This was an all-time low. I had finally scared the shit out of myself. I drove the rest of the way home frazzled, windows down, pinching my cheeks while thinking "I just need to make it home and get to bed."

During the train ride to work I kept replaying the night in my mind. I knew I smelled like a piss-tank, I could feel the booze sourly coming out of my pores. Keeping a low profile at work, I messaged my boyfriend. I felt sheepish, trying to blow it off as no big deal when I told him about falling asleep at the wheel. I was really starting to care about him, so I don't know why I chose to share this irresponsible thing I did with him. He didn't answer for a while, and when he did he just responded with "Nice."

Later that day he wrote me an email. He expressed that he was concerned about the decisions I was making lately. He signed off with "How does someone so smart do such stupid things?"

For some reason that really stung. My heart raced and my face flushed from shame. That one sentence made me feel so many things. I felt scared, thinking he might leave me because I was just 'too much, too reckless,' I felt like an idiot but at the same time I felt a tiny bit of hope, because he acknowledged that I might actually be, dare I say, smart.

I felt like I had disappointed him and myself... again. Sad that he saw that side of me, touched because he might genuinely care. I felt like if I didn't smarten the hell up, I would sabotage yet another good thing with someone I actually cared about. I felt like this man, that I was falling hard for, took the words right out of my mouth. Words I have repeated to myself thousands of times over the years. Words that struck so deeply because I knew that they were true. Obviously I know better than to drink and drive because it's just wrong and um, hello... it's the law. But I am smarter than that so why did I do shit like that? Why did I continue to do such stupid things when I know I'm smarter than all that nonsense? I felt like this message was so loud and clear, like a smack across the face. Not the usual "you are such a moron!" facepalm. No, this was a "JASMIN! WAKE THE FUCK UP!!!" bitch-slap.

Frankly, I was getting tired of my own bullshit. I had been feeling this way for a really long time but it seemed to be coming to a dangerous head. I would have these amazing moments of feeling really empowered, intelligent and even proud of myself. I knew I had the capacity and desire to do bigger things, greater things, impactful things. I knew there was an ambitious wise woman in there somewhere. I've proven to myself repeatedly that I have the aptitude for success, between my street smarts and surviving on my own at sixteen to my ability to excel in school.

Yet, there were many times I willingly participated in situations where I was left feeling physically or mentally crappy. But I continued to repeat the same behavior. It was as if I didn't have an 'off switch', even when I would say to myself "Jasmin, you know better than this. Pace yourself man!" Unfortunately common sense would leave me and I'd be drawn to the excitement, the rush, the attention, the moment. I would completely forget the pep talk and rationalize why it was okay to go out, make out, drop out, whatever 'out' was intriguing in those moments.

Inwardly I would constantly berate myself with negative thoughts about how much I sucked, I'm not a worthy friend or girlfriend, I'm lazy, I'm a procrastinator, I'm not good enough, I don't measure up, my legs are gross, my ass is huge, my hair is stupid, I'm stupid and on and on. I often playfully referred to myself as 'damaged goods,' except I wasn't playing. I would then flip flop and outwardly express with gusto "I am my own woman, I do what I want because I want to. No one is making me do anything! I'm a free spirit man! Fuck it, you only live once!" I meant it... all of it.

I was so convincing I even believed my own tall tales! Strangely those powerful statements are still true, but they were so misunderstood in my misguided disempowered mind back then. I realize now that I was actively choosing the drama, the immediate gratification which was a form of numbing out. I was ultimately causing new emotional pain to escape my old emotional pain. Talk about a mindfuck. It was like trading fire ants for yellow jackets. It was time to truly do the work and be accountable to myself.

The Work. What does that even mean? Accountable. Now what does that mean? Before this tipping point I was already very aware of the burden of my lack of self-worth, self-confidence and self-love. Just prior to this rude awakening, an amazing woman loaned me this self-help book called 'You Can Heal Your Life' by Louise L. Hay. I finally decided to investigate this concept even though I was terrified of picking my emotional scabs which had been festering for far too long. I had to at least try to do the work to see if change was possible. Could it be any more terrifying than the path I was currently on?

The 'work' began with simply becoming aware, especially in tougher moments. Noticing my negative self-dialogue, I would then try to be kind and compassionate towards myself. Taking stock of my self-worth. Owning the responsibility for my actions that resulted in me feeling bad. Pausing the old program, the gut response. Trying to hold and love me in all my unpleasantness. Choosing thoughts and actions differently. Finding new approaches for healthier ways of being. Baby steps. Explore what my driving force was when making shitty decisions. Reflecting and questioning if what I was telling myself was actually true. Choosing my next move from that compassionate space.

From this kinder perspective I now could ask myself if my thoughts and actions were helpful or harmful for me. I wanted to be a better person, the one people already believed I was, but I didn't.

Sounds like a lot of fucking work, doesn't it? It was harder than I thought it would be. I realized that I was locked up in the prison of my own mind and I had the key all along.

With that self-help book, I finally found the right vocabulary to articulate my inner conflict. It was my first awakening of many on my journey to understanding my actions, while guiding me beyond the stories. There were over twenty years of experiences, conditioning, grooming and observing that lead up to this breakdown and wake-up of self. The book couldn't save me from two decades of programming. I actually had to do the 'work.'

Most importantly, I learned that I had to be the one to save myself from rock bottom because no one else could. I was done with being afraid of feeling vulnerable. I was tired of the white lies, stretched truths, blurred boundaries and sabotaging my own life. Where do I even begin? How do I pull all those old stories apart? Pen to paper was the first step I took. Journaling helped get the noise out of my head and to be a witness to my own thought patterns.

I had to unwind the events of my 'Jerry Springer' life. How did I become this social, care-free, workaholic, hypersexual, insecure, self-loathing, comedic, non-trusting, loving, kind, hard-shelled, frustrated and dysfunctional woman? To know me, you likely wouldn't have realized I struggled deeply and internally with my dark shadows. My moral code and standards were distorted. I had been 'acting out' most of my life and at times it even looked like being 'empowered'. How does that even happen?!

I was wondering what was one of my biggest challenges and where did it stem from? I began to explore past experiences that were personally profound in hopes that I could discover where I was blocked.

Growing up in one of the sketchiest parts of Toronto, Ontario in the late 1970's, gave me some valuable street-smarts as a child. We were taught to avoid the passed out, piss-stained drunks in the stairwells and elevators of our twenty-two story building. An unwritten rule was to be leery of the 'bums' and the 'glue-huffers'. In other words, pay attention to our surroundings!

Although we lived in the 'hood', I had a pretty great life. I played with my friends, ran the roads until my dad whistled for us to come home, had affectionate, colorful hippy parents and was taught that manners were mandatory. Although we were a low-income family, my parents made efforts to take us on fun trips to parks, tobogganing and camping.

Those were the days when sending your six- year-old to the store for milk and smokes was acceptable. On my way home one day this man started talking to me. "Hey girl. You like chocolate bars?" His accent was so thick that I almost couldn't understand him. I assessed him and figured he was okay to talk to. "Yes please." I said with my best manners. "Just reach in the bag. You need to move things, the chocolate is under those things." he said. I reached into the bag that he was holding in front of him and all I could see were bars of Irish Spring soap. "Keep looking, they are at bottom." As I reach in again the man lowers the grocery bag that's been against his body to reveal that he's fully exposed and erect. I clearly remember being shocked and frightened. I ran screaming home to my daddy as fast as I could. I've never forgotten the smell of that Irish Spring 'pervert soap'. I now knew that I should not trust unknown men and about 'stranger danger.'

I distinctly remember a conversation with my parents when we were camping one summer. They shared this helpful life-tip with us. "Your grandfather will be watching you guys for a few weeks while we stay here. He can be a little too touchy-feely. If your grandfather tries to do anything to you, you just tell him NO and that you will tell on him if he doesn't stop." I am now thinking of times when he babysat us in the past. So are you saying that the long baths, the getting washed a little too thoroughly, the sitting on his lap in a towel in the dark watching television felt odd to me for a reason? Or are you saying that when he'd wake me up in the night to offer me treats in exchange for touching me 'down there' that was too 'touchy-feely?'

Although relieved that I could now tell him NO, I couldn't quite understand why they would leave us in his care in the first place. I didn't ask questions. We were taught to respect our elders, especially our parents. At seven years old I was confused to learn that I needed to protect myself and that I could not always trust my grandfather's intentions towards me.

The winter of 1983, our parents decided to move us away from the 'Big Smoke' Toronto. They found a very affordable hundred year old house in a quaint town where I went into third grade mid-year. That year was awesome! We all made new friends, we were safe to bike everywhere and we swam almost every day. This was a far cry from my city living experience! My dad still worked in Toronto as a delivery man, while my mom kept up the house and garden. He'd travel back and forth, sometimes staying in the city to save on gas.

One particular spring day my dad announced that he was heading to the store to get smokes. The day turned to night as hours went by and he didn't return. Mom thought maybe dad headed down to the local arcade to play video games. This shouldn't have taken him more than an hour tops. Mom was trying not to be alarmed. She thought maybe he was visiting our cousins across town but when she called them, they hadn't seen him. Mom called the hospitals and walked all through town but nothing turned up. My siblings and I had no idea what was going on at this point. Mom chose not to call the cops as she suspected he just needed a little space. What us kids didn't realize at the time was that our parents had been having trust and fidelity issues for a few months prior to all of this.

We didn't hear from dad for weeks, not even a phone call. I assumed he was just working in the city. Mom was really struggling to keep things 'normal'. After the three weeks of leaving mom with three kids, no car, job, or source of income, he finally decided to come home. Just to announce he was officially leaving. I always thought mom and dad were playful, affectionate, and deeply in love. I was shocked to see such coldness in my father as he was my idol. I had never witnessed my mother so vulnerable, frantic, stomping and screaming obscenities.

It was becoming clearer by the second that what dad meant was that he was also leaving all of us. Watching him pack, while helplessly seeing my mom in a complete meltdown crisis was a turning point for me. This was the defining moment when my inner light was dimmed and fear of the unknown entered. This was my first heartbreak.

It was like a switch was flicked and very quickly everything went to shit. I felt puzzled that my hero would do this to us. I thought I was his 'baby girl'. In just over a year of moving to this rural town we became both a broken and financially broke family. Everything I knew to be safe, secure and true was no longer a truth. It was becoming clearer to me that I cannot trust men, not even my own father.

I understand that it's difficult to pinpoint why my parents' relationship started to waiver. We were oblivious to the issues between them. There were several muddy layers to this story to sort through. What I do know for certain is that things got steadily more unstable over the next few of years. My mother cried all the time as if she was mourning. She was devastated like someone died and took my sparkly mother with them. With this sadness came new behaviors for all of us. My sister acted as our guardian, my brother became the man and the muscle of the house and at nine, I was now the security blanket my mom would hold on to, cry on and talk to. Soon after my father left it was learned that he had developed a relationship and moved in with my mother's closest friend. She was like an aunty to us kids. While she became my stepmother, my mother became a drinker. I understood that loyalty and commitment are but a suggestion, not a presumption. I'm discovering that it's not always safe to trust even your closest friends. People have ulterior motives.

After my dad left, mom starting seeing an old childhood friend. The unfamiliar man came into the picture as this big, energetic, charismatic and classy guy. He seemed loving, affectionate and generous. I thought he was going to save us. We quickly discovered that he was wonderful, until he got into the booze. He would then become jealous, violent, and destructive. After his raging outbursts, he would then sob apologetic tears of remorse.

Both my mom and her boyfriend started drinking more heavily. His explosive episodes were becoming more physically and verbally abusive towards my mother. His eyes, his tone, his erratic behavior would shift. Punching holes in walls, calling my mother names, smacking, shoving and pinning her down in front of me. He didn't care that I was right there. By ten years old I knew not to trust men in general. You can't trust people when they drink. You need to be on guard because you can't trust anything to be predictable, stable or safe. Mom is not safe. I'm not sure mom can protect us anymore either.

By eleven years old, I was continuously experiencing unsettling situations. However, sadly it was becoming the new norm. We were so broke we were burning furniture, a guitar, and random wood from our yard for heat. We had even turned on the oven, leaving the door open. Paying for basic necessities such as hot water, food and laundry supplies was becoming a challenge, we also had our phone cut off. I couldn't trust that my mom was still able to properly care for us and our basic needs. It felt really troubling that I couldn't trust that we are going to be okay.

My mom was hitting the bottle pretty hard on a daily basis. I also started partying, drinking and smoking pot around thirteen years old. Life was moving along and I was evolving along with it. I was boy-crazy, hanging with older kids, stealing food, lying and not giving a shit about my grades or attitude. I was self-harming by carelessly piercing my own ears twelve times using blunt dirty studs. I felt rebellion coming on; developing thick skin due to the hardship of poverty combined with the heaviness of puberty.

My brother and sister both moved out at sixteen. Mom and I bounced around several places, finally ending up on a foam mattress sleeping on the floor at my extremely religious, very French grandmother's house. By eighth grade I had gone to five different schools and was lovingly deemed 'The Devil's Spawn' by my grandmother. I knew I had to escape this unstructured, insecure life with my mom, so I moved in with my dad and his new family at fourteen. My dad shared the news they were expecting. What? Are you having a fucking baby? But I'm the baby! All the fun dad stuff pretty much stopped at this point.

By ninth grade I had become increasingly edgier, riskier, self-reliant and street smart, so I found it very difficult to live with parents who wanted to 'parent' me. Not being used to rules and restrictions, I moved out that same winter. My nineteen-year-old sister took me in until tenth grade. We both realized that this was just too much to expect her to do. I reluctantly moved back in with my dad, as living with my alcoholic mother was not an option. Once again I moved to another town, another school, another set of friends to make, another kick at the can with being a family unit. That lasted two years and I still felt trapped. Although grateful they took me in, I moved out at sixteen years old.

By the time I graduated high school I had attended twelve schools, fifteen if you count college, and I managed to earn a scholarship with honors. I worked multiple jobs and collected student welfare to get by. I lived with a few boyfriends. I fell in and out of lust and love. I developed many friendships. I was becoming closer with my siblings and was always trying to maintain a relationship with both parents. I struggled at times between doing what was right or choosing more risky, impulsive behavior. I was discovering the craft of being a woman and how it can work in your favor. I honed many 'survival' skills over the years from having to read situations and people.

Reflecting back to all the times I should have been able to trust certain people, I realized that they had all on some level manipulated, exploited, neglected, disappointed, confused, made empty promises or expected me to keep their troublesome secrets. These experiences evolved into self-sabotage. I believed trust, honesty, and loyalty didn't actually exist. I didn't want to be the victim in my experiences because I felt that was weak or helpless. I was a warrior (don't you know!) but sadly I was groomed just enough to believe some experiences were either my choice or my fault. I would own some situations that weren't fully mine. I was too afraid to let people in, to trust anyone fully and had a protective wall up. If you gave me reason to mistrust you, I'd cut you out. Then there would be these mindbending moments when mentors or allies came into my life and showed me that amazing things were possible, even for me! The problem was I didn't fully believe these people, because I didn't trust them. I was waiting for their angle.

Everything always seemed so jumbled but then it finally hit me.

That saying, 'follow your heart.' How could I follow my heart when I didn't know how to trust what it was saying? I realized I had a false sense of self. Trying to see myself other than as 'damaged goods' was really hard. I didn't feel like I was 'enough' of the good stuff. I realized I was afraid of success in all avenues of life and I felt unworthy of it. My behavior supported this belief.

With coming to terms with my perceived self-limiting beliefs, I wanted to lean into what I was willing to do about it. How did I want to show up in my life?
I didn't want to feel unworthy.
I didn't want to feel like a party favor.
I wanted to stop the noise in my head.
I wanted to have deep, meaningful, safe relationships.
I wanted to be open to vulnerability and personal growth.
I wanted to understand healthy boundaries.
I wanted to learn forgiveness, let go of judgment and have compassion.
Fuck the fear of playing small, of saying NO, of offending others.
Fuck being afraid of trusting good people, of intimacy, of respectful relationships.
Fuck the fear of having a loving, trusting relationship with MYSELF.

By twenty-four years of age, I was in a healthier position, where I wanted to open my heart to possibilities. It felt very challenging and risky. I've had tastes of what that might feel like but it scared the crap out of me. The only person I completely 100% trusted to always have my best intentions was my big sister. My close friends truly loved me but I wasn't allowing myself to fully believe it. I had past boyfriends but they wanted to control me, tame me. My last boyfriend was a kind loving man but didn't know how to handle me as I was still filled with dysfunction and drama. He left me and I don't blame him.

My next boyfriend, the one who called me out on my poor decision making bullshit, became my husband. He taught me how to love myself without even meaning to. I had just started the process of working towards self-acceptance, so I felt I was in a good place to learn. He taught me about self-respect, self-care, boundaries and being authentic without the head games. He is honest, supportive and loves me unconditionally... damaged goods and all. He made me feel worthy by showing me that he felt worthy and respected himself. He is my mirror, my guide, my rock. He is a straight shooter with loving intentions. He is the healthy example I finally trusted.

Over the years I continued to study self-improvement material to stay plugged into my healing. I worked really hard on practicing compassion, understanding and forgiveness towards myself and others. There was a lot of journaling. I finally TRUSTED my heart. I attended massage therapy school and have been an RMT practitioner among other healing modalities for eighteen years. I now understand why my heart longed for this work, offering unconditional care and healthy touch. I have a livelihood that fills my soul, while working on my empowerment coaching program where I can guide others.

I have developed the most incredible healthy relationships which have helped me evolve. The more I come to terms with the shameful moments of my past, the more I expand. When I'm aware my internal dialogue is consistently positive, I'm joyful. The times I allow people to hold space for me, I feel supported unconditionally. When I acknowledge my grace through the hardship, I'm moved to tears. I have come to trust my feelings, my choices, my relationships since I've chosen to be transparent. I feel my vulnerability has given me strength and is setting me free. I feel safe and worthy enough to authentically be my playful, empowered, lovable self.

Continuing to trust my passion, I have become a mentor on empowerment, self-love, mindful connections, authentic expression and genuine joy. Since my awakening twenty years ago, I haven't stopped practicing or exercising my 'true north heart center' muscle. It feels like blossoming, like intuition, like deep growth. I hope my experience inspires others to give themselves the courage and permission to say, "FUCK FEAR" and prosper. I warned you it was hard work but it is so worth it. You are so fucking worth it!

I've never felt this healthy before
I've never wanted something rational
I am aware now. I am aware now.
~Head Over Feet: Alanis Morissette

Jasmin MacKinnon has owned Sogo Body Therapy's wellness studio since 2004. She specializes in Registered Massage Therapy and Licensed Body Sugaring Hair Removal but has a multidisciplinary toolbox of therapies. Jasmin has an innate desire to treat and mentor her clients. She is expanding her profession to include Empowerment Life Coaching and mind-blowing collaborations with heart-centered folks. She facilitates Women's Empowerment retreats and co-created YouTube's meaningful yet comical #mouthymamas vlog.

Jasmin is playful, truthful, and reflective in all areas of her life. She resides in Nova Scotia with a husband she adores, her two inspiring children, and her juicy cat.

Ultimately we know deeply that the other side of every fear is freedom.

~Marilyn Ferguson

Cheryl Martin

Breaking Free

All I wanted was to be loved. To be appreciated, valued, respected, cherished. Nothing more, nothing less.

At 16 years old, I was a typical teenager. I enjoyed school, loved choir practice and boys. So when I was dared to wave to a cute boy on the city bus, of course I did! Could a boy like him be interested in me? Regular, ordinary, nothing special me? Yes! And so it began.

I stepped into my first relationship with innocence, I was hopeful, naïve, and trusting. The first warning of what was to come happened only a month later.

I was visiting Paul at his mother's house. We had an argument, feeling a little hurt, I got up and started packing to go home. I had planned to take the last bus home at 11:00 p.m., even though it was too early, now seemed a good time to leave.

Angry and hurt, Paul asked "Where are you going?" "Home." I replied. The tension was high and I wanted a little space, however Paul insisted I was not leaving without him escorting me to the bus stop. I just wanted fresh air and space, so I quietly said "I am going alone." Suddenly I found myself being shoved down on the bed, hard. "You are not going alone!" he sneered into my face. Something inside me recoiled and tears sprang to my eyes. Instantly Paul switched from angry and menacing to soft and apologetic. Sincerely he begged me to forgive him. Shocked and confused at how quickly the whole thing happened, I let it go and stayed, until that last bus.

It wasn't long before it happened again. Paul saw me hug a male friend at school and called me that night accusing me of cheating on him. Convinced, he refused to listen to anything I said. Steaming mad he punched his hand through a speaker, slamming down the phone, breaking it. I was desperate for him to understand, I had not betrayed him. I called back, again and again, until finally his sister answered. She blamed me for his outburst. "It's all your fault Cheryl." *How could it be my fault?* I thought. *I hugged a friend! I did nothing wrong. He broke the phone, not me!* I sat there silent as he came back on the phone. He was not going to listen to me anyway.

In the first few years, when conflict arose, I did what I had been taught as a child, kiss and make up. One of the important values that had been instilled into my core was forgiveness. I forgave so deeply I forgot the pain. I chose to keep all the good and happy moments, storing the sad and rage-filled moments deep in my unconscious, putting them in box on a shelf, never to be opened again. I believed what I was doing was healthy and the right thing to do.

At 19 years old, I was finally free and off I went to spread my wings at university. But unlike most students, whose memories are of parties, coffee shops and late night chats on threadbare chairs in dodgy apartments; my most vivid memories were of me, sitting in my walk-in closet, on the phone. Half the time laughing, half the time crying, and staying up until the wee hours trying to resolve whatever 'hurt' Paul was feeling.

Within weeks, he was accusing me of cheating and I was miserable. Every move I made was questioned. Every knock on the door, every hour of my evening had to be accounted for. I began weighing the choices in my head. If I went out to dinner with my friends, what would I tell him? Often it was easier not to tell him anything.

I quickly learned, no matter how many questions I answered, he was always waiting for me to slip up. He kept looking for the details of my story to change, so he could pounce on it, to prove I was lying. Loving him deeply, I questioned my own behavior, started tightening my reins, paying attention to everything I did and everything I said. I would have done anything to not hurt him.

Just like any other abused woman looking back, the signs were all there. All of the things I had been accused of, had been present in Paul's past when he was a little boy, in his parents' relationship. Despite his efforts and steadfast commitment to "not turn into my father," the beliefs, behaviors and values he had been exposed to had become ingrained into who he was. Just like my naïve belief that forgiveness resolved every problem.

Unconsciously, to avoid the hurt and rejection he felt as a child, Paul was driven to create in me the very same sense of urgency and desperation, to ensure that I would never leave him. Like his father did to his mother.

It worked. Paul created his reality and I accepted the role he gave me.

Throughout my college years it escalated. Constant questions, discussions (aka lectures), all eroded my sense of self-worth. Whenever I started to feel equal and confident, the scales would tip. Sometimes while we were out I got 'the look.' His eyes would narrow slightly, he bit his tongue, stiffened his jaw and I knew some sort of verbal tirade would happen on the way home. It threw me off balance, and I would spend the rest of the evening quiet and withdrawn, reasoning out in my head what I had done wrong and how to smooth it over.

Separated inside myself and weighed down by dread. I watched while he, and the rest of the world, laughed joyfully, unaware of the chaos I was feeling. It seemed he would go looking for something to get upset over sometimes, just to set me off balance again.

The night I graduated from university was memorable, but not for the right reasons. After a celebratory dinner with my sisters, we all headed to a local dance club. I felt amazing and I was excited to dance all night.

Then it started. Placing his hand on the back of my pants Paul pulled the waistband closer to my skin and growled into my ear, "You should wear a belt. You know better." I had heard this before, so anticipating his disapproval I had checked to make sure my shirt covered the small gap in the waistband of my jeans. I had forgotten about dancing though. As he sat by the bar, brooding, I danced with my sisters half-heartedly. Most of the time, I was watching him, waiting for his mood to lift a little, planning out how I could fix this. In my head I was frantically trying to save my big night from the disastrous argument I knew was coming.

I put on a fake smile as I sat down beside him. I was anxious. As I sat there listening to insults and snide remarks about how I was tempting other guys to look down my pants, I began to doubt myself *Was it true? Could I have really done this on purpose? What's wrong with me? It's not true!* I argued with myself. Confused, I tried to hug him. He pushed me off and went outside to smoke.

I followed him outside a few minutes later, distressed and hoping he had blown it off. "Come back in and dance with me?" I begged. Tears streamed down my face. Four years of University, the first member of my family to earn a degree... and it no longer mattered. He argued with me in the street, gesturing wildly and yelling. I was so ashamed and embarrassed, I hid myself in the hollow of an adjacent storefront doorway.

My sisters stepped in to reason with him, but he wouldn't listen. Only his pain mattered. In the middle of the main street, in front of my sisters, on the most important day of my life, Paul broke up with me, got into his truck and drove away. Abandoned.

Later, while my sisters and I got ready for bed in our hotel, a sick feeling spread in my stomach. Part loss, part fear and all dark and twisting. As they fell into sleep, I lay there anxiously, in heightened alert, listening to their breathing and for the rumble of Paul's truck. I prayed he would come back. For hours I lay there suspended, barely breathing, almost frozen. Somewhere around 5:00 a.m., I drifted off.

At 7:00 a.m. Paul banged on the door and stormed in, demanding I talk to him in his truck. Like a chastised puppy I followed him outside, silently accepting his tirade and the blame for his suffering all night in his truck. The voice in my head repeated over and over *it was his choice*, but attempting to block his angry yelling also drowned out the voice.

As I packed up my stuff, I felt uneasy. I knew I was betraying my sisters by leaving them, my sisters who had stood beside me while my heart shattered and picked up the pieces. What I didn't realize was that I was betraying myself too.

From that day on, the trajectory of my whole life changed. I pulled away, folded myself up trying to fit the mold Paul expected. I hid away the parts of me that didn't align with making him happy. Whenever my inner voice spoke up, I silenced it, stuffed down the hurt, and the protests. Instead I presented a facade, a mask of who I really was inside. Nobody knew of my pain, nobody heard the inner screaming as I went against my own judgment. And I believed I was happy.

Things got better, for a time. We camped, painted the house, built a garden and adopted a dog. They were happy times with regular days and I began to wonder if I had made it all up. When he called me names, insulted my cooking, complained about dog hair on the clothes, I thought that it bounced off like rubber, when really it was glue. I made excuses for him, "He had a bad day."

Occasionally my emotions would rally, so I would respond with a snide remark defending myself, but it was short-lived. *Isn't there conflict in every relationship?* I reasoned. My thinking became so scrambled I believed I deserved the onslaught that came every time I spoke up for myself. And still we moved forward with our lives, got married, bought a house and had a child.

It started out as a small rash on my thumb. A little patch of eczema, or a contact rash from poison ivy. By then I was back working full-time, taking care of our daughter, the household and still getting no help at all. Whenever I was feeling stressed the rash flared and became itchy. With Paul's constant criticism, insults and general disdain for my existence, it began to spread.

In two months, it progressed to covering my legs, upper thighs, around back to my buttocks and every part of my torso. It moved into my hands, making every effort painful from the combination of itchiness, swollen fingers and water blisters forming and popping. It hurt to make dinner, wash the dishes, take care of my baby. Everything was super itchy, like I was trying to escape my own skin. My hands were raw, cracked and bleeding. I couldn't sleep because of the constant raw pain where my body touched the sheets. It spread up into my scalp, where the oozing blisters caused my hair to fall out in patches. Now I was ugly too.

What I didn't realize then was that my body was screaming for my attention. I was being verbally and emotionally abused, mentally controlled and manipulated. My wild soul was being squashed, stepped on, held down and underneath it all I was drowning.

I was in complete denial. Paul's projection of his own beliefs onto me was so slow and subtle, that I bought into them. I believed every word he spoke, every move he made to intimidate me, every time he laid his hands on me in anger, would all roll off of me. It didn't.

My body was sending me a message. Deep down at the core, my unconscious mind was protecting me. My body had manifested this rash, covering 75% of my whole body.

First, to alert me that something was very wrong, and second, to ensure that Paul would never touch me, in love or in anger. And it worked!

I was so deep in denial, that I became two different people. Away from him, I was myself, cracking jokes, being silly, playing pranks and having fun. Sometimes, when he saw this woman, we laughed and had fun together. It made me hopeful.

But, underneath his laughter, he boiled. Waiting until we were in the car to chastise me, claim my sisters were manipulating me or accusing me of flirting with my male coworkers. I fought hard to defend myself, but nothing I said would change his mind. Again, he "knew what he saw."

That's when I withdrew from my family. I gave up. Even with a 1-year-old daughter, I kept my family at a distance. It made sense inside my head, I was protecting them from his wrath and judgment, protecting myself from losing them. I isolated myself. It was a lose-lose situation for me anyway. I denied the abuse. "I'm fine." The excuses now were about me. Nobody could help me, I was stuck. Almost a year went by without seeing my own twin sister. I retreated into a shell. I stopped being me.

"Because when you're in the thick of things, in the middle of a Hell that you're convinced is of your own making, you can't see

anything clearly. Fear and shame consume you—they're your
constant companions. And when you look at your family and
friends, you often can only see judgment and derision.
You know their opinions about women who stay in
abusive relationships."
~Janice Fuller-Roberts

It only got worse. It was midnight and my child was crying. He followed me up the stairs, antagonizing me, standing over me as I lifted her. In the chair I rocked her, trying to calm her. It wasn't working. I couldn't calm myself. Inside my voice screamed, *Get out, get out! Leave us alone!* But I couldn't say a word.

He stood there in the doorway brooding until I begged him to leave so I could settle her. He still respected her enough so he did. But her little body was tight. She knew. I rocked her long after she fell asleep. Already she had become a shield between us, a tool. I couldn't protect her. Torn, I kept rocking. It was not just to soothe her anymore, was it?

I heard him coming up the stairs again. The fear dropped into my belly as I quickly placed her back in bed. Standing in the doorway, he blocked me in. He started again quietly, mocking me, making it my fault she couldn't sleep. I needed to escape. I slid past him into the spare room. He followed me. I wanted to go to sleep, block it out, but he settled himself in the bed, challenging me to withdraw. I felt suffocated, pressured. When he tried to touch me I flinched and then pulled away. It was instinct.

My rejection hurt him and again his voice got louder and he resumed his attack. He followed me into our bedroom, berating me, quietly through clenched teeth and taut shoulders. His fist was closed and pumping, again his body blocked me in. The quietness of his voice triggered a cold sweat, this wasn't going to end well. I escaped to the spare room. No matter which way I went he would follow. I was trapped.

Again the baby cried. He stood in her doorway, not letting me in. "Mama!" She cried harder. With tears in my eyes, I begged him to let me go to her. I felt myself crumble inside, as parts of me slipped away. I was failing her. He picked her up, sat down and rocked her himself. She calmed a little, still calling for her mama.

I stood where she couldn't see me and motioned for him to give her to me. He refused. I didn't understand. Was he taking it personally because she wanted her mama?

When she wouldn't stop crying he handed her to me, holding onto her little legs possessively for a few seconds longer. He won't let go. Was he trying to hurt me by withholding her? It was past 2:00 a.m. and my eyes burned from all the tears.

I paced the room with her as he revealed his plan for a trip 'back home.' I was not invited. It was a veiled threat. When he demanded I sign for her passport, I felt my heart fall to the pit of my stomach. Up and down my emotions went.

I was relieved when he finally announced that he would leave for the night and stay at his mom's. Pretending to say goodbye to Sophia he grabbed her and ran down the stairs. I swallowed fear and panic.

As he sat on the stairs struggling to put our crying child in her winter coat I packed her diaper bag and dropped in some snacks. Tears fell silently down my cheeks. With a quick kiss and "Mommy loves you and I will see you soon" I turned away. I couldn't watch as my child was taken from me. I had no fight left. Letting her go was the only way I could protect us both.

I heard the screen door click behind me. I burst into sobs. I felt my soul being torn from my body. There was nothing left. And then, his voice came from behind me as he stood at the front door, "How could you think I would ever take her away? You're so stupid."

In that moment, a decision began to form. Not consciously, but deeper. Over the next couple of months I began paying attention to my body, noticing my gut reactions. The numbness wore off. Instead of shrinking into myself or disconnecting, I stayed conscious. Allowing myself to see what was really happening, to feel the anger and the hurt from his barbs.

I began to feel guilt and regret; recognizing how long I had allowed myself and my beautiful daughter to be disrespected, taunted and intimidated. I allowed it to fuel me. It was clear the relationship was at a breaking point.

He must have known it as well. His behavior toward me swung back and forth between desperately loving me and furiously despising me. For the first time ever he asked me what I wanted. It was too late. Fifteen years was a lifetime to invest and I was beyond empty, gutted, done.

The point of no return happened one weekend in early June. After days of escalating threats and berating, I found myself not only fighting for my freedom, but for my life. My only thoughts were to stay alive, to protect my child. I fought and kicked and screamed. I tore myself from his grasp, from his hands pinning me to the bed, from his hands around my throat over and over again. This time, it was me who escaped outside. I heard the door latch close and I never looked back.

I began to put the pieces of my life back together. My daughter and I, who was not quite three, moved in with my mom. We settled into a routine with Sophia spending equal time between her dad and I. Focused on creating a parenting relationship, I did what I believed was best for our daughter and continued to placate any conflict that arose.

Many who have not been through a domestic violence experience believe that getting out is the end. It's not. The abuse continued. Disparaging comments about my parenting escalated to accusations and calls to Children Services. Despite my attempts to create a fair environment, he twisted every word I said.

Again, he went after my throat, threatening to take Sophia away. On the outside, he was calm and collected, everybody loved him. Only myself and those who had witnessed my abuse could see his inside, where he continued to seethe with anger, resentment and revenge. To make me pay.

Aware now that the abuse was going to continue, it was time to ask for help. Growing up with a strong, independent single mom, I believed that asking for help made you weak. I had spent years doing everything myself, took pride in it even, and here I was barely able to hold myself together. I couldn't even wash my daughter's hair! Not asking for help became a problem.

On the outside I wanted everyone to believe I was doing okay, I was a survivor right? And that is exactly what I was doing... surviving. For every step forward there was one step back, sometimes more. My world was falling apart and I was the last one to notice.

So I took the first steps. I hired a lawyer to fight the court battle for me. Then I sat down with my boss. As I told him my story, tears streamed down my face. I felt shame burning my cheeks. In his eyes though I found acceptance and compassion. Able to breathe once again, I felt hope for the first time in forever. Finally, I made the call to the women's shelter counseling program. I asked for help, for both Sophia and I.

The first pivotal moment came on the second day of class. There were six of us sitting in the circle. I was nervous, like a taut bow with an arrow loaded. As we took turns reading about the cycle of violence, I held myself in check, stuffing down my adverse reactions and listening quietly.

Then it was my turn to read. I opened my mouth and choked it out, intimidation. My voice shook, faded out and cracked, but I pushed on reading. Tears formed in my eyes until I couldn't see the page. I didn't need to. The last sixteen years of my life was intimidation. I felt a hand on my shoulder and looked up to see tears in the eyes of the other five, including the counselor.

Knowing what had happened, in my head and in my body, was one thing. Saying it out loud made it true. "I WAS ABUSED." There is power in truth. For the first time in sixteen years, my voice spoke my truth.

I continued to put myself back together. I found support, guidance, strength and courage to ask for what I needed. I made time to be myself, to spend with friends and family, time to heal. I spent an entire summer floating from cottage to camping trip to backyard BBQs, feeling free and whole and myself again.

And as I healed, layer by layer, I invested time in understanding the dynamics of abuse, codependency, and how I personally contributed to my pain. I delved into researching and reading, learning again who I was and what I needed to be happy. Instead of fighting for control and giving until I was empty, I learned to receive.

To make sure that I had created trust in myself, I practiced with my male friends, accepting their offers of help. By allowing myself to BE, to actually experience my feelings and accept them, I no longer stuffed them inside.

Regardless of all the work I had done and all my efforts to heal, his manipulative behavior continued to trigger me.

Each time I heard his voice switch into fake sincerity I cringed inside. When Sophia came home telling me about the way her dad repeated himself over and over until she stopped protesting his punishment, it was like I was zapped back into the past and it was me who melted into silence.

I tried to explain to counselors, but their only advice was to use positive affirmations and for me to treat him the way I wanted to be treated. Deep down I feared I would always be stuck with this anxiety and dread. How was I to co-parent and stand up for my child if I still couldn't stand up for myself?

The answer came as an invitation to a networking event. I met up with Laura, a friend from high school. She didn't get two minutes into her story before I felt something crack inside my chest and a cry burst out of my mouth. Laura was an NLP practitioner and as she described how negative emotions and traumatic events were stored in the body at the cellular level, I started shaking.

What she promised was a way to release and forgive all the trauma I had been through. To free all the emotions that rose up, sending me into panic or rage inappropriately. To release the insults and judgments I thought I had let go of, but that continued to erode my self-worth.

I sat there dumbfounded, with a new understanding that I could be free. My skin began to tingle and hope swelled inside.

Weeks later I saw Laura for my Quantum Change Process session. In three hours I let go of more pain. I found deeper depths of healing and forgiveness than I had been able to with three years of traditional therapy. Parts of my past memories, limiting beliefs about myself and what I truly deserved, all these thoughts that had been stuck inside me unconsciously, were released.

I floated down her stairs and over to the kitchen table barely able to contain my excitement. I knew without a doubt that this was a missing piece to my own healing and to my life's work. My eyes twinkled and I laughed loudly as I claimed confidently "I am supposed to be doing this work, how do I get trained?"

Three years later I continued my healing journey and obtained a full toolbelt of techniques to help others as well.

Along the way I have been challenged and as each layer came up for resolution, I asked for help. I continually deepened my understanding of why I had chosen this path. Piece by piece, I retrieved the broken shards of me, my courage and my self-worth, putting myself back together. Building myself back to wholeness.

And yet, the cracks will always remain, the places where I am different, where the experience has expanded me. They are the places where the light shines through.

"I am not what happened to me.
I am what I choose to become."
~Carl Jung

Life has a way of breaking us. Only we get to choose whether we are broken, or broken open. Either way, it will hurt. The truth is, pain changes us. That IS its purpose, that IS the meaning of life; to break, to grow, to expand, to become more.

So as I fill these gaps with new beliefs and new behaviors, they become the places where I am the strongest. Your deepest wound, I say, becomes your power. And I chose to have it become my purpose too.

After her experience working with an NLP coach to reconcile and learn from her abusive past, **Cheryl Martin** founded Soul Spark Coaching where she is an expert in resiliency and Post-Traumatic Growth. Cheryl uses her suite of skills including NLP, Hypnosis and Timeline Therapy, to guide her clients through the process of change at quantum speed, to release past hurt and trauma, let go of negative emotions, build new beliefs and behaviors and reclaim the life they were born to live.

Don't be afraid to go out on a limb. That's where the fruit is.
~H. Jackson Browne

Nadine Matejuk

In Charge Of Your Destiny

Searching for the right partner is like eating a bunch of grapes. We carefully select the one that most appeals to us and get ready to enjoy the succulent sweetness. If we're lucky it slides down effortlessly... not so lucky and we'll bite into it just to find that it's sour, tasteless or just plain rotten!

With movements such as #MeToo and #TimesUp, society has totally aligned with my methodology from over 35 years ago... as a strong unit, women can together accomplish anything!

ENGLAND

My family headed off on a vacation to England for three (*3) weeks when I was fourteen years old. How exciting to be going on my first plane ride! Our trip consisted of visiting my mother's aunts, uncles, cousins, friends so we hopped from one household to the next. The memory of our trip from a teenager's perspective consisted of three (*3) distinct memories.

The first was that it rained all of the time in England. The second was that English folks eat very little, but always seem to have a lot of silverware at each place sitting. The third was that it was the first time I felt violated, shocked and uncomfortable as a young woman.

During our family tour, we visited my mother's friend and her husband for dinner one evening. While we were saying goodbye and hugs were flying about, the husband came up behind me, cupping both of my breasts in his hands giving them a firm shake. I hoped he meant to hug me and that his hands 'just slipped.' I felt a weird numbing sensation run through my body that made me extremely uncomfortable.

Looking back I made the mistake of not mentioning it to anyone else, especially my mother, as it was her close friend's husband. It wasn't until decades later, when my mother received a note from her friend informing my mother of her husband's death, that I spoke up and spilled the beans on that dirty old man! Obviously, being the young woman that I was, he wasn't a 'chosen grape' but he definitely chose me to try his shenanigans on!

I knew what he had done was wrong, so I promised myself as a young woman that it would be the first and last time someone was ever going to get away with something like that. Our three week trip ended up being lovely. But unfortunately this remained one of the unpleasant highlights. Looking back, if the movements on social media had been around back then, maybe I would have realized how wrong his actions were and I would have spoken up much sooner!

THE CHICKY CLUB IS BORN!

From the age of sixteen, when I was away from home and had my first summer job working at a lodge, I knew that I would have to put on my big girl pants. I had to become my own independent warrior, without my mom and dad around to watch over me.

Being the social butterfly that I was, I quickly established a close group of friends or 'Chicks' as we called each other. We had each other's back through our blast of teenage crushes, lodge romances and drama. The four Chicks became each other's warriors. It was my first exposure as to how our girlfriends could inspire, empower and support each other. Especially in the absence of our parents over the summer months. Our club continued for two additional summers between each school year. These three (*3) other women still remain in my life thanks to Facebook! Little did I know at that age how important 'Chicky bonds' would become for me. How the close females in my life would become my rocks for the coming years.

FLORIDA

I was nineteen years of age when I boarded a plane with my girlfriend for a week of sun, sand, fun and as a dance teacher... lots of dancing!!

With the bass of the music in my chest and the sexy, low glow of the nightclub, we were excited about what adventures the night had in store for us! As I scanned the crowd, my eyes were instantly drawn to the tall, dark and handsome man with the moustache that resembled Tom Selleck in his earlier days. Being the romantic that I am, I leaned over to my girlfriend and said, "See that handsome guy over there, I am going to marry him one day!" To which she replied, while rolling her eyes, "Yeah right." As our eyes locked, we made our way to the dance floor. A couple of dances later (perhaps melting his heart with my trained yet flawless dance moves) we spent the balance of our holiday together, along with our respective friends.

I received love letters, handwritten in calligraphy, by mail as there was no internet back then. Plane rides back and forth, long distance phone calls and visiting at our parents' homes. A year or so later we announced our engagement!

BOSTON

I was only twenty-one when we married. My parents drove me to Boston, the trailer filled to the brim with my most prized and decorative possessions, to set up our first home together. Reflecting back on those days, I realized I was fairly courageous to leave the comfort of our family home and head to another country without my family or my Chicky friends. Love could conquer any fear! Neither of us really knew anything about living outside of our family homes. Hell, we thought the toilet paper just magically always appeared on the toilet roll! We had so much to learn together.

I managed to get a job teaching dance classes and choreographing dance routines for a reputable dance studio. This kept me busy for six days a week, providing ample opportunity for my husband to find 'other interests,' including our travel agent.

I will never forget the feeling, sitting across from her, while planning and discussing the details of our honeymoon. While she was presenting hotel options, she was literally staring directly at my fiancé, peeling her clip-ons from her ear lobes and playfully throwing them on the table. Without losing eye contact with him, she slowly removed her blazer revealing her cream sheer blouse. "Are you for real? Is anyone else watching this?" I thought to myself.

I'm not a jealous person and quite secure in my skin, but this was so blatantly obvious that my jaw was literally hanging down, my mouth wide open in disbelief. When I brought this to his attention, my fiancé said "Don't be silly. Are you becoming insecure now that we're getting married?" For a couple of years the travel agent continued to call our home, asking for my then husband to get on the phone. My reply to her was "If you have specials then send us marketing literature. I'm sure you don't call every client to inform them of special offers do you?"

Well needless to say, the phone calls stopped but my stomach told me that my three (*3) plus years in Boston were up. I secretly saved my 'runaway' money and enough to rent a U-Haul from working extra waitressing jobs through the day. I had been naively handing over my paycheck from the dance studio to my husband every two weeks. The thought of a separate bank account hadn't entered my mind, as I thought this marriage would be my forever fairytale.

The fairytale soon ended when reality crept in. Discussions, tempers and Scotch whiskey don't mix well with men in general. I was also missing my family and hometown Chicks, which only added to that mix. Even my friends at the dance studio couldn't replace the love I missed from my family and friends being away in a different country.

So I began my plan to depart. Slowly I packed up my things. My husband was shocked one day when he came home and found seventeen boxes staring back at him. He appeared unfazed, as if I was bluffing, right up until he saw the U-Haul outside of our home later that week. My sister flew in from Toronto and with every possession I had packed away, we 'cheered to independence' with our subs. We drove from Boston back to Toronto as I prepared for my next chapter.

I must admit that I knew my hunches were correct when I left that day. Because shortly after, the travel agent in her sporty Fiero car, arrived in our driveway and never left. In fact, they married and had two beautiful children.

In hindsight, things worked out the way they were meant to. They shared many years together before they too parted ways. My ex-husband unfortunately passed away last year.

It brought chills to my bones and the hair on the back of my neck stood up when I heard that his three (*3) ex-wives (me being the first), were all coincidentally in Boston on the night of his passing. The only night I had been in Boston, while on a layover, in the twenty-six years since the day I left. RIP my dear friend. You were a good man but we were just too young. You were my fresh new grape off of the vine but perhaps I picked you much too early!

JAMAICA

A few years later... it was a beautiful sunny day for a wedding in Jamaica. With one failed marriage already under my belt, I was excited to start a new chapter in my life. Yet, my chakras were conflicting with each other. My heart felt love but my biological clock was belting out 'tick tock' encouraging me to make a silly decision. My gut told me it was time to get married, so I could raise a family, but the logic in my head was questioning my decision. What was I fearful of?

When I met the tall, Steven Segal lookalike bodybuilder at a dance club in my hometown, he put his hands in the prayer position and said "Will you please dance with me?" Oh Lordy, do you see a pattern here? I must stop going out dancing and meeting these celebrity look-alikes!!! After three (*3) years of dating, he proposed to me in front of fifty of our friends on New Year's Eve of the millennium. What a night that was! Year 2000, a new year and now a new marriage to come!

On the morning of our special day and suspicious of my demeanor, my sister pulled me aside to ask me if I was really certain about continuing on with this special day. To which I replied "Our family and friends came all this way for a wedding and they're going to get a wedding!" She told me that I didn't have to do it if I had doubts. She even suggested that we could run away to another resort or leave the island for a couple of days, until everyone got over the shock, should I decide to cancel.

If this was a TV show, it would have been an episode of 'Survivor' but how would I have known at the time? With a keen desire to begin a family, I decided to move forward with the 'I do's' not realizing what lay ahead for me. I guess at thirty-seven years old, I still gave a shit what people thought if I changed my mind and I didn't want to disappoint anyone.

Coming home from our destination wedding after three years of dating changed everything. The short skirts that he loved while we were courting were now too short. Regular dance nights with my girlfriends became "Where are you going?"and "You and your f*cking girlfriends don't have to go out every weekend!" Yet I was told to "Mind your own f*cking business" when I questioned strip club receipts that he left around. My Chicky friends, whom we once hung out with, were no longer nice people in his mind. The five course meals that his mother made each day for him made my attempts at various new dishes appear less than satisfactory.

One day I was excited and attempted to make homemade Fettuccine Alfredo for my new hubby. Rather than commending me for my efforts, he belted out "This tastes like shit!" So I grabbed his plate, threw it out and walked away in silence. Silence was powerful and soon became my new friend. This was totally out of character for a chatterbox like me!

In addition to focusing on my career and squeezing in five workouts a week, I had the added responsibility of being the wife of a 230 pound man. He was 6'3" and built like 'The Rock' on steroids! Each day became my living hell as I realized that the man I married was lacking some basic moral values. During my two months of hell, my state of happiness swung back and forth like a piano metronome. In his mind I was either "the most beautiful woman in the restaurant" or I was a "f*cking bitch" because I stood my ground. I was growing tired of the constant verbal and emotional abuse that was thrown my way on a daily basis. I even tried to forget the feeling of his strong grip on my shoulders when we had a disagreement. He pushed me against the wall, leaving imprints on me like children's handprint pictures.

On a side note, my father who was a World War II Veteran (bless you in heaven Dad) always wanted his children to be prepared for anything, at any time, in an effort to protect us. My father spoke many times of how we are always in charge of our own destiny and how we should never feel stuck or helpless in any situation. He would teach us self-defense and quite often he would say "If someone is grabbing you like this, how do you get out of it?" Then we would demonstrate our escape from that headlock or body clutch. He would always remind us "If anyone attacks you, never let them know you're scared!" This coming from a man who had often said "I would cut off my finger to make your mother feel safe and happy!" A true war hero and forever our protector!

One evening, at around (*3) a.m. my then husband received a message from a drunk friend who happened to be a girl. I told him "While I don't mind you having female friends, now that we were married, your friends have to respect the fact this is our home. And now that we are living together, we can't be bothered through the night with this drunken foolishness." Thinking this was a normal request, I was shocked at how quickly the night accelerated into one I would like to delete from my memory file. His reply verbatim was "Well you're a f*cking whore!"

What?? Did I miss something? I'm here sleeping with my husband and I am the whore? WTF?!! We were married for just over two months and he had become a different man. I wanted the emotional, verbal and recent physical abuse to stop! I wanted to be loved by my husband, not feel disrespected. I was a bright independent woman who certainly deserved better!! My immediate shock turned into anger and then 'never let them know you're scared' the teachings of my war hero father came into effect.

I decided this was fight or flight. Well I confidently chose fight and what followed resembled that of a WWF TV event. In disbelief, I clenched my right fist and hooked him, punching him on the left side of his temple. I must admit that it was satisfying to see him fall back until he quickly rebounded. He placed his left hand around my neck while he threw me on the bed and drew his right fist in the air, similar to pulling back on a bow and arrow. "My face is going to be officially mangled" I thought to myself.

While I wanted to cry inside, words of courage flew out of my mouth and I yelled at him, staring him directly in the eye "If you're going to raise your fist to me then you better f*cking hit me!" What the hell was I thinking shouting that out? I guess I was hoping that my father's advice would work by letting him know that I wasn't intimidated. I was hoping to keep my face from becoming mashed potatoes. Thanks to my Dad, he quickly realized I wasn't afraid, got off of me and swiped the top of my head as if flicking a fly away from a meal. When I got off the bed and walked toward the hall, he grabbed me by my already bruised shoulders and threw me on the marble bathroom floor of my condo. How the hell did I end up on my left side checking out the baseboards? "Oh that hurt and there's going to be bruising" I thought to myself. Then the girly girl in me turned total Hulk when I realized that the red nails on my left pinky and ring finger were broken. I was really pissed thinking "How do I explain this to my nail technician?" I heard the condo door close and my bully of a husband was gone. Thank f*cking God!!

Once I got a grip on my emotions, the little girl that learned defense tricks from her Daddy came out and took over the resilient tough warrior that the world knew. Tears poured into the palms of my hands and I found myself on autopilot, dialing my parents' phone number. Within an hour they were at my place and I told them about the two month nightmare of this shit show called a marriage.

By early morning, I cancelled his entry card for my condo, had the locks changed and called my understanding boss to explain that I wouldn't be at work that day.

My dad preached the power of being in charge of your destiny and it has always stayed with me. We are never stuck in any situation and there is always a way out. Thinking that this grape would be a nutritious one, it displayed its bitter, rotten and tasteless attributes once I peeled the skin back!

I truly do respect the spiritual principle of Karma. The joke was on the bully when I served him divorce papers on April Fools Day! Sweet revenge was mine!

LIFE ENCOUNTERS & LIFE CHATS

A couple of years later, I found myself enjoying some pleasant time with a handsome, intelligent gentleman, filled with stimulating conversations and fun outings. When my mother met him for the first time, she said to me "I feel like I've seen those blue eyes before and there is something so comforting about his eyes." Yes, the universe always has better events in store for us. Like the arrival of our beautiful daughter! We decided to raise our darling daughter together, but apart, and are amazing friends to this day! Coincidentally, similar to what my mother was feeling, our daughter has those stunning blue eyes!! Figuratively speaking, one could say that good things come to those who wait and this grape had longevity and made wonderful wine!

Fast forward over a decade and I found myself in a profound conversation with my one and only little girl. Instead of putting my daughter into 'defense' positions like headlocks, similar to what my father would do to prepare us for attackers, I had chosen to consistently ask her questions to prepare her mentally.

The chats with my young girl went something like this "Honey, what would you do if a man yells at you or touches you inappropriately?" She would reply back with the optimal answer of "Throw him to the curb!" Then I would ask "Why?" to which she'd favorably reply "Because there's plenty of fish in the sea!" Wahoo...Woot! Woot! Yes, we have success!!!

These conversations would periodically and repetitively occur over the years just to make she always remembers the ideal solution!! Shine on and stay strong my love... shine on!

BERMUDA

Years later there was no nightclub, but I was still dancing! This time aboard a yacht in Bermuda! Standing alongside my Chicks with the hot sun beating down on us and Rihanna blasting from the speakers, I saw a uniformed officer drive by on a police boat. My heart skipped a beat when he flashed those pearly whites at me and waved. I was curious to see his eyes behind his aviator sunglasses. He approached our boat. I'll never forget his presence when he stepped off his boat in his black boots, to show off his rope knot skills while tying his boat to ours. Having gone through his own personal hell with two failed marriages, fate would bring us together to share our similar stories. We both invested many hours, sharing over FaceTime chats and visits before we both decided to give it a go and together tie our own knot! I had finally found my soulmate!

This was a third (*3) marriage for both of us. So 'third time's a charm!' I became a wife again but this time took on five stepchildren. A different dynamic from my first two marriages. I thought it was difficult moving to a different country in my twenties, however, the courageous one this time was my daughter. Moving away with me in her preteens, as we changed the dynamics of our family from a small and close knit one to a much larger one filled with unknowns couldn't have been easy for her. Exposure to a different culture, new school, new step-siblings, on a little island in the middle of the Atlantic versus the big metropolis of Toronto was a huge change for her! Blending families isn't easy.

My daughter comes by her strength naturally from the strong women in our family. After all, even her grandmother (my mom) left her husband in the 1950's when she wasn't happy. At a time when all the other women were greeting their husbands at the door, with slippers and newspapers in hand, she went on to marry the love of her life... my father, until he passed away.

My daughter wasn't happy in Bermuda, verbalized her discontent and wanted to return back home. Proudly, she stood her ground and did just that. Even though I tried to please everyone by constantly flying back and forth, my heart ached and I just couldn't handle being away from her. My heart was back home in Toronto where I could be with her and my family. It was where I wanted to be. So that is where I returned.

My husband and I have been married for three years now, back to our long distance FaceTime chats and talks about what the future holds. Only my personal angels and the higher powers know. All I know is that home is where your heart is and that all of us are in charge of our destiny, just as my father told us for years.

Along with those wise words, I have additional thoughts that I carry with me. Over the decades, I've learned we should never give one person the power to define our happiness. It doesn't change the past, but it does change the future and the freedom to live the life we deserve.

We all have scars and we all have fears, but never be afraid to love and to believe in love.

The only way to heal is to have faith in yourself and learn to trust again. As I once heard "Strong walls shake but never collapse."

No one is perfect. I've learned to forgive others and myself for mistakes that are made, by releasing the emotional blocks of things in the past, in order to keep my load light. If we carry those emotional negative blocks with us from the past, it will only provide significance in our present. When we learn to forgive, we become stronger and that is very empowering.

A struggle we are battling today is developing the strength we need for tomorrow. We either learn lessons or we change. For me, it was both. I have slowly over the years developed my own wish list or rule book of what I will accept and what I want from various relationships. I've also learned that I can depend on myself and be my own warrior as I refuse to live in fear of anyone.

Also, when a number consistently shows up, as in my case the number three (*3), I realized that there are patterns in life. Besides disliking uneven numbers, I also needed to peel back more layers of my own onion and have a closer look. There's no time like the present to do some serious journaling, self-inquiry and make positive changes in our life. We are never too old to change for the better!

My mother would constantly remind me to be accountable for my own actions. When I was a little girl I had a little autograph book that had all of my family and friends' signatures in it. They all wrote their own words of wisdom. For some reason, what my mother wrote has always lingered in the back of my mind:

"Your future lies before you like a path of driven snow
Be careful how you tread it for every footstep will show."
~Author Unknown (but in my mind it's my mom's quote)

The strong females in my life, our shared Chicky chats and the power of sisterhood has remained in my life over the decades. It has now grown to include many countries all over the world through... The Chicky Club.

My wish for you is the same. Honor your family and friends, give yourself the permission to be an endless sea of transformation, be accountable for your actions and walk proudly in your skin. Strive to feel balanced and centered and live without fear. Oh and I almost forgot... if life gives you a raw deal while you're searching for your partner, put your fears aside and have the courage to keep eating those grapes!!

Nadine Matejuk is the Founder and Director of The Chicky Club— A fun online group that supports, inspires and empowers women through their own personal journeys. Nadine has a background in dance and is currently a yoga and spinning instructor outside of her 29 years in the corporate world. Nadine also runs her company Enhance It Interiors as an Interior ReDesigner, Stager and Color Specialist.

Nadine is a mother of one beautiful daughter and lives in Ontario with her family. Nadine is thrilled to finally put pen to paper on some of her experiences to share and bring people together!

You can conquer almost any fear if you will only make up
your mind to do so.
For remember, fear doesn't exist anywhere except in the mind.

~Dale Carnegie

Janice Pavicic

Breaking the Chains

Whenever I smell lilacs, the memory comes flooding back. I am hiding behind the lilac bush in our backyard. Cindy, my faithful protector, a medium size German Shepherd licks my face. I can hear the smashing of dishes and a lot of screaming and crying. My dad had that voice, that when he yelled, you just cowered. He was scary, very scary when he was drunk, which was every weekend and most weeknights. Every Friday my mom would pack me in the car and head out to my aunt's house. We would stay there until Sunday afternoon and then head home, just to have it start all over again.

Some people tell me they have memories of their childhoods going back to when they were just infants. I remember bits and pieces, but mostly chaos. And the yelling, always the yelling. The bad memories never leave, they come again and again, when a smell hits your nose or a song plays on the radio. I remember the fear of hearing the back door slamming when he came home from work late, after going to Duffy's Tavern for drinks.

Many nights, mom would sleep in my single bed with me. For years I thought she did it for me, but thinking back I think she did it because he would very rarely come and pick a fight with her if she was in bed with me.

Until one night, my dad came stomping through the house in what seemed to be the middle of night. She left my bed and got up to try to calm him down. Minutes later the screaming started. It was pretty loud that night so I got up to try and stop him. As I rounded the corner of my room I glanced into the kitchen, I can still see her, sitting in the chair, his hands wrapped around her throat, he was choking her and she was fighting him.

This was the first time I can remember challenging my dad. I think I was about six years old and I just started screaming for him to stop, hitting him with my fists. He turned his anger on me. The look he gave me was all I needed and I ran.

I called my older brother. He was twenty years older than me and lived with his girlfriend. I begged him to come and make it stop. I wanted him to take me away. I can still feel the shag carpet under me as I sat on the floor in my room. I can see the black rotary phone and I can hear his voice, telling me everything was going to be okay. That daddy would stop soon and go to bed. My brother didn't come that night, I cried myself to sleep.

My brothers were 17 and 20 years older than me so they had moved out years before. Every year, or two, they would resurface, moving back home for awhile and then leave again. They had endured many years of this before I was even born. But I always felt jealous that at least they had each other. I had no one.

Mom and I were very close as I grew up, two peas in a pod you could say. She never went anywhere without me, looking back I guess she really couldn't. So instead, in 1976 mom packed our bags and we moved out.

Funny, I don't have any recollection of actually moving, but we ended up on the top floor of some huge old house. We got two separate bedrooms and shared a kitchen and a living room with three others. We were there for about six months and then we had to leave, I have no idea why. We then moved to the top floor of my grandma's old house. I had my own bedroom and my mom slept on a couch in the kitchen.

My mom started attending Al-Anon meetings on Monday nights. She told my father we would not come home until he quit drinking. I have this cloudy memory of visiting my father in the hospital but no one would ever tell me why he was there. I found out years later that he had swallowed a bunch of pills after we left and tried to take his own life. Shortly after this incident my father quit drinking. He never drank again.

A few months later we moved back home. Years later and on several occasions my mom would tell me that she only moved back home for me. She never wanted to go back, but I kept begging her to go home. She did it for me. She never let me forget... she did it all for me.

Sometime later I was whisked off to stay with my mom's friend Auntie Linda. My mom had another nervous breakdown and my dad dropped me off and told me he'd be back soon. It was January 1979, my tenth birthday was approaching and all I wanted was to be with my mom. I couldn't call her because she wasn't allowed to have a phone.

It was hard for me to go anywhere and stay overnight because I always peed my bed. My mom told me it was because I had a small bladder. Even now at 49 years old, as soon as I get anxious, I feel the heat rising slowly up my body, my heart beating out of my chest. The fear rises and I instantly have to pee. The yelling and screaming always started at night and I would lay paralyzed in bed most nights too afraid to get up and go to the washroom. I spent at least four other times away from home, when my mom had 'nervous breakdowns,' that's what they called them then. My mom was given several prescriptions to help her deal with her depression/anxiety and took them for years. It angered me that she would just keep stuffing those pills down her throat and then check out mentally. She would sit at the kitchen table smoking and drinking coffee for hours.

Goodbye Daddy

In 1999 my father (22 years sober) passed away suddenly in his sleep. He had been sick with a cold, and I was visiting to check up on him. He said he was tired and wanted to lay down. I tucked him in bed, squeezed his hand and kissed him goodnight.

Later, at home with my husband, I told him I thought my dad was going to die that night. I had this terrible feeling. Everyone thought I was crazy. The next morning the phone call came, my mom couldn't wake him, he was gone.

I had forgiven my father a long time ago, the last few years of his life, he was very different person. He seemed to have no memory of the horrible things he had done to us. We think he was having mini strokes as we would sometimes find him on the ground in the backyard. He never seemed to know how he had gotten there. He would drive someplace and forget how to get home. He refused to go to the doctor. The years of abusing his body had finally caught up to him.

I wrote the eulogy for my father's funeral. His death hit me very hard. Memories came flooding back, conversations I wish we could have had. Questions remained unanswered. His childhood wasn't easy. My grandmother had become a violent alcoholic when he was just a little boy. His sister passed away at the age of two from scarlet fever. She drowned her grief with alcohol for many years and took her pain out on the rest of her family. She eventually found AA but the damage had been done.

Granny Goodwitch I called her. She had long flowing grey hair and was quite a character from what I remember. She rolled her own 'ciggies' and was always very kind to me.

My oldest brother had forgiven my father and had a good relationship with him the last few years he was alive. But my other brother hated him and was relentless in conveying this to him. Every birthday, every Christmas, every holiday we all walked on eggshells waiting to see if he would show.

One of my earliest childhood memories is visiting my brother in the 'hospital.' I am about three years old and I am doing a plastic puzzle on a hard metal table, across from me is my brother wearing blue pajamas. I am scared of him.

He acted nice to me sometimes, but mostly he was mean. He had crazy eyes and he laughed a lot. My mother denies taking me to jail to visit him but I remember very clearly the bars on the doors and the white walls. My brother saw the inside of many jail cells over the years, as well as Queen Street Mental Hospital for drug addiction and mental health issues. He was a very violent drug addict and alcoholic that constantly rained terror upon our family.

When I am ten there is a banging on the front door in the middle of the night. My mother answers and it's the police. They have my brother Steven in the back of the police car and they don't know what to do with him. So they bring him home. He is clearly on some type of hallucinatory drug. Angel Dust (aka PCP) was his drug of choice back then. He thinks he is Michael the Archangel, and wants to tell the world about it. He has a mental illness.

This is the 70's so they didn't know how to handle mental illness very well. My mother doesn't want him in the house and she asks them to take him somewhere else, but they refuse. My father can't deal with him because he is afraid of him too. My brother starts smashing his head on the windows in the police car so loudly that my mother starts screaming. I am standing in my housecoat begging them to let me go to him. I want to go to him. I want to help, I know I can.

No one is watching me and I walk to the police car in my bare feet. I stand and stare. My brother is smashing his head and his fists against the windows. He wants out. I am frozen in fear. Time stands still. His rampage continues into the next day. I am watching Saturday morning cartoons in the living room. He comes storming out of his bedroom and yells at me to turn it down. I made the mistake of yelling back at him. He runs towards me, picks the television up off the floor and throws it through the front glass window of the house. I am frozen, terrified again.

Years and years of anger and violence from my father are now replaced by my brother. There is never peace in the house. He terrorizes us on a regular basis. I lived in fear most of my childhood, in fear of the men in my life who are supposed to love me the most. It's no wonder I entered into an abusive relationship with my first boyfriend when I am sixteen.

The first time he slapped me we were walking home from a party and we were both high. The abuse continued on for ten years as we eventually moved in together.

There was one difference in this relationship from the one I witnessed as a child. In this relationship, I fought back. When he hit me I would never run from him, I challenged him head on. Dared him to hit me harder, and he did. I would hit him back. I continually wore long sleeved shirts and turtlenecks to cover the bruises.

In 1994 the police were called by the neighbors after he threatened to throw me off our balcony. The police put us both in cuffs because I had hit him back. They agreed not to press charges if we both consented to counseling. It was then that I made the conscious decision that this had to stop. I would not live the same life as my mother. The violence and destruction would end here. It was like I finally woke up .This is when I started my healing journey.

I started doing evening classes at the local college, selling a women's clothing line and doing home parties. I found my old passion for reading. I took public speaking courses and got out to meet new people. And I started dating, something I have never really done because I had been with my partner since I was fifteen.

The truth is, I met my husband while I was still living with my partner. Something stirred in me that had never been there before. He was kind and gentle and treated me as no other man in my life ever had. With respect and love. His presence and the love I finally felt gave me the strength to move on with my life.

My husband and I married in 1997 and we had a little girl in 2001. Life couldn't be better. I was finally free of the old patterns of pain. I had very little contact with my brothers. We were never close.

Mom

My mother and I were always in contact. We spoke on a daily basis. I always told people that my mother and I were best friends, two peas in a pod. We were so close and we meant the world to each other. Looking back now it seems it wasn't really true. It was what I wanted to be true, but it wasn't. Funny how the more you tell a story, whether it's true or not, the more real it becomes.

My mom had taken prescription pills since before I was born and continued to take them through all of my childhood. The thirty plus years of taking antidepressants, anti-anxiety and even antipsychotic pills had taken their toll.

After we buried my father in 1999 she started to change. We were slowly trying to get her off her daily regimen of pills, it took almost a year to wean her off completely.

She started having strange side effects from the pills. She would stand up and sit down literally hundreds of times a day, saying she couldn't sit still. She started having strange mouth movements and jerking limbs. She would spit up never ending mucus and would barely eat. She was losing weight fast. At one point she would only eat banana and peanut butter sandwiches, nothing else.

When I asked her questions she refused to answer. When I tried giving her alternative options she refused. I took her to homeopaths, naturopaths, neurologists, geriatric doctors, specialists, psychiatrists, healers and more. Nothing helped, no one had any medical explanation. I knew it was the side effects from taking the pills for more than 30 years. It had affected her nervous system and done permanent damage.

The hardest part was taking my daughter Lilli to see her. Lilli would try to get her attention and all mom would do was sit in the goddamn rocking chair and stare into space. Truthfully I was so angry at her. "What the fuck is wrong with you?" "Why can't you try?" "Why won't you talk to me?" All she did was stare back. I was heartbroken and furious all at the same time.

After years of my trying, our phone calls became further apart. I would call and she wouldn't talk. I would still visit her weekly, keeping myself busy cleaning the apartment, as it was becoming filthier and filthier by the minute. She would not clean and she barely washed her clothes. There was hardly any food in the fridge except for TV dinners, ketchup and chocolate. Food was slopped on the walls, the floor, everywhere. This was not the way for someone to be living, it was so unhealthy. So I tried to talk to her about getting someone to come and help. Of course she refused. She got worse and worse.

I had not been in contact with my other brother for almost 10 years at this point and I decided to reach out to him. I wanted him to talk to my mom about getting her help. I thought we needed to pull together as a family and try to get her somewhere safe. Somewhere she could be monitored, have clean surroundings and most importantly have people around. She was becoming more and more isolated. This plan backfired.

The day after I spoke with him I called my mom and she hung up on me. I called back three more times and the same thing. On the fifth call she answered and told me to never call her again. She told me she knew I wanted to 'put her away' in a home and she wanted nothing to do with me. I tried to talk to her, but she would have no part of it. I tried visiting her that evening and she would not answer the door. I tried for every few days for weeks, but she would not even hear me out.

Unbeknownst to me, both my brothers had been living off my mother's money since my father had passed away and the house was sold. If she went to a home then the money would stop. So they decided to tell my mother that I was up to no good, that I wanted to put her in a home and take away her freedom. They lied and it broke my heart. I tried for months to call her, I told her what this was doing to my daughter. She wanted her grandmother. My mother literally said "That is too bad." Apparently, the mistakes I had made were unforgivable. She let me know that we would never see her again.

I went into a deep depression, I cried daily for weeks. I cried for the mother I lost and the love I never received. I could not understand how any mother could do this to their child. I cried because all I ever did was take care of her. Not the other way around. "Don't cry you might upset your mother." "Be quiet your mother is sleeping." "Don't bug your mother she's not well." I wanted my mommy and she was gone.

I tried to move on but couldn't. Earlier that year I had started my own business and was so excited to pursue my dreams. Everything had been going so well, until this.

In July 2012 I woke up one morning and could not move my neck without excruciating pain. I had no idea what happened to cause this. I thought it would pass, but it didn't. Days turned into weeks. I saw chiropractors, healers, doctors, physiotherapists and nothing helped.

Stress takes a physical toll on the body and you never know how it will come to the surface. I believe the pain of being disowned by my mother all these years finally came to the surface and I had to feel it, to get through it.

The doctors offered me oxycontin. I refused to take it. With my family history of addiction there was no way I was going down that path. Turns out I had a herniated disc, but there was nothing they could do about it. It didn't require surgery, it had to heal on its own.

I believed it would not heal until I made peace with the fact that my mother would no longer be a part of my life. I had to let her go. It took six months. I cried almost every day and night. I barely slept because of the pain. I meditated, prayed and somehow got through it. One day I just woke up and it was gone.

"Pain travels through families until someone is ready to feel it."
~Stephi Wagner.

And boy did I feel it, in more ways than one.

On November 23, 2014 I received a call from my niece. My mother was in the hospital and it wasn't looking very good. My brothers, of course had not told me this. My husband and I went to the hospital that evening. As I entered the room I couldn't believe my eyes, my breath left me and I almost collapsed.

In two years my mother had deteriorated to a tiny little lady that I barely recognized. She was literally skin and bones. Her hair was wild and her eyes were clouded over. Any part of the woman I once clung to was gone.

I entered the room and approached her, not knowing what kind of response I would get. She looked up and smiled. She did not know me. I spoke to the nurses and told them that I was her power of attorney. I had the papers with me.

My mother had been brought to the hospital because she had fallen. She basically did not have the strength to walk anymore. Her legs just gave out. Considering she weighed about 85 pounds now and was basically a skeleton I can imagine she had barely been eating for months. The nurses came back and told me that my brother had a more recent power of attorney that trumped mine. Of course he did! I would have to go through him to get any further information. My mom had changed her will too.

Over the course of the next month and a half I visited my mother every day and stayed with her for as long as I could. I knew she was dying and I wanted to make peace with her. She hallucinated most days but there were moments of lucidity. I crawled into bed with her as I had done for many years as a little girl. I held her hand and told her that I loved her. The blessing was that she forgot why she was mad at me. We never spoke of it. She saw visions of my father; she said he was coming to get her. The worst days were when she saw a black hole and screamed because she was falling. These episodes sometimes lasted for hours. It was exhausting for her and for me.

The day before she died I came to the hospital to find her almost glowing. She looked radiant. At the time we thought it strange, and for a moment we thought she might be getting better. We talked for quite awhile and she told me "it's time to face the facts" that she was not getting better. And then in an instant her eyes clouded over again. She started panicking and told me she had to go. "Please let me go Janie, please let me go!" she begged. The nurses gave her something to calm her down. I whispered to her that she could go, that I would be fine.

I was very upset and told her I would come back later. I didn't go back that night, I just couldn't. Something told me to stay away. The next morning the nurses called at 6:05 a.m. and told us to come to the hospital. She was already gone when we got there. It was a gift that I got to spend that time with her before she died. While taking care of her it helped me to heal the wounds that were so deep in my soul. The connection between a mother and daughter is so deep that it can never be broken, even in death.

I still feel my mom and dad around me whenever I need to talk to them. I loved them dearly and miss them both. I believe that I chose these people to teach my soul the lessons I needed, to learn to evolve into the person I am today.

I am proud of the strong woman that I have become, that I am still becoming. We are all faced with struggles and challenges in our lives. Coming from a family caught up in addiction and self-destruction, it would have been so easy to choose another path in my life.

I am a work in progress and the journey of healing is a long road. But the chains of addiction and violence can be broken. The chains end here.

Janice Pavicic is the owner of Healthy Living Plus, a retail Health Food Store in Toronto. As a survivor of domestic abuse and generations of addiction, she uses her experience and education as an Addiction Counselor and Reiki practitioner to help others along their healing journey.

She is currently working on her certification as a Registered Holistic Nutritionist and resides in Etobicoke, Ontario with her beautiful daughter Lilli, amazing husband Tony and two fur babies.

Courage is not the absence of fear it is the conquest of it.

~Anonymous

Erin Pellow

Just One Thing

Put your hand up if you've ever cried at work. Yep, me too, more than once. A colleague saw me crying one day and actually started to laugh. She was quick to apologize and assure me she wasn't laughing at me. She simply didn't know what else to do. She had never seen me like this. I had always seemed to have it all together. Then I started to laugh, if she only knew. I wish I could tell you a story about how I had it all together. Offer you some words of wisdom. "Skip to the end," as my Dad would say. But I haven't reached my destination, I'm still figuring things out. And yet, this is an important story, because it's about how I took that first step. How I did just one thing, and how it changed everything. How I put aside a good life, and paved way for a great life.

Growing up, I followed the prescribed checklist for someone of my generation. I did well in school. I was well behaved, polite, and responsible. I worked part-time during the school year, and over the summer to save money for university where I graduated with honors. After university, I spent two years living and traveling in Europe. I moved back home and got a job, sometimes two. I even earned my master's degree while working full-time. I did everything I was supposed to, and by all accounts, I was killing it.

I remember my 'pump the brakes' moment. I was in a meeting with my manager at the time, and she said to me, "Given your chosen career path..." what came next, I don't recall. I didn't hear another word. What did she mean chosen career path? I did not choose this, well, not on purpose anyway. I was just biding my time; putting food on the table while I figured things out. I liked my job well enough, and I was good at it, but surely, this was not where I was going to end up. This really got me thinking, and I started re-examining my life.

I saw my friends becoming established in their careers as teachers, lawyers, business owners, and other fancy things I didn't understand. They were getting married, buying houses and having kids. It all seemed to be coming together for them in lockstep. Meanwhile, there I was working a job, still pondering a career, single and not really loving it, renting a crap apartment, with all of my children safely on lockdown as unfertilized eggs in my ovaries. WTF? This is not what I thought I was signing up for. I followed the path society had laid out for me, and I guess I thought eventually, everything would fall into place. Except it didn't and I'd be lying if I said I wasn't deflated. Was this some kind of joke? Did I miss a memo somewhere? Did I zig, when I should have zagged? Where was my dream job, my husband, my house, and my 2.5 kids? That's what I was working for, wasn't it?

I don't know about you, but once I start comparing myself to others, it can be difficult to stop. That social media rabbit hole, you know the one, where you get deeper and deeper into highlight reel after highlight reel. It started with people you knew, and suddenly you're browsing the lives of complete strangers. Then the inner dialogue starts. "Oh hey, negative emotions and limiting decisions. You wanna join this party?" I don't want to get all Anne of Green Gables dramatic here but next thing I knew I was in the depths of despair, lying on the floor hoping Mindy Kaling would come feed me sour straws. Cue more jokes and obscure pop culture references.

Things had sure escalated quickly. I just couldn't help myself. We learn to compare at such a young age. Growing up we're taught to put the square block through the square hole, to identify which group has more and which has less, to compare and contrast. It's how we learn to choose, to compare features and prices, how things taste, how things look, and how things feel. It's how we learn to evaluate. What were our profits year over year? How do we measure up against our competitor? Who wore it better?

There is nothing wrong with comparison, in and of itself. The problem with this comes when we assign value to those comparisons. Up to a point, it's all about similarities, and differences. It's just information, mere data, and yet, at some point we decide to apply meaning to it. When more or less equates with good and bad, that's when things get muddy.

Society encourages us to assign value to our comparisons. As adults we are tasked with keeping up with the Joneses. We look at magazines and we see instances of people being caught out. Look at these celebrities who have cellulite, who look different without makeup, and who struggle with relationships. These articles aren't attempting to normalize these facts, they're not reminding us we all struggle with the same things. No, it's an attempt to assign value, to make them less than. And if those attributes are somehow less than, and if I share those attributes, I must be less than as well. It's not true, but sometimes it feels like it is.

This is when you need to remind yourself to take a step back, to look at the bigger picture. You see, the funny thing was, those lives I was looking at and comparing mine to? I didn't actually want to live those lives. Not really. Those careers didn't interest me. Was I looking for a life partner? Absolutely. I was prepared to be selective on that one. If I owned a house, I'd be tied down, I couldn't just pick up and leave. And are you ready for this? I wasn't even sure I wanted to have kids. Bold statement, I know. The lives of my friends and other random strangers weren't better or worse than mine, they were just different.

Around the same time as this vocational crisis, I was introduced to author and speaker, Danielle LaPorte. She asked brilliant questions like, "Can you remember who you were, before the world told you who you should be?" Uh... no, no I cannot. I had spent so much time focusing on what I should be doing, I didn't stop to think what I could be doing, or even what I wanted to be doing. I read LaPorte's book *The Desire Map*. It explored the idea of creating goals based on how we wanted to feel rather than what we wanted to accomplish. What a novel idea.

I wanted a life that lit me up, a life lived with intention. I wanted to spend my days connecting with people, inspiring them to live out their dreams. In turn, I also wanted to continue to be inspired to live out mine. I wanted to explore new places, and feel enriched by learning new things. I wanted to share my experiences and knowledge with others. I wanted a life full of laughter and joy. I wanted to celebrate the big things life has to offer, and be enthralled by the little things too often overlooked. I wanted to live a life with an outpouring of love. Love for myself and love for others. I wanted to share every bit of this with my great love. Someone who would brave this journey with me, and amplify the best of me, just by being the best of him. I wanted to feel beautiful. I wanted to be passionate, and sensual. I wanted a life of vulnerability, authenticity, and acceptance. I wanted to be able to give, so I could truly understand what it meant to receive. I wanted a life of abundance and nourishment. I wanted to feel a sense of accomplishment. I wanted to jump out of bed in the morning refreshed and excited for the day. I wanted to go to bed feeling fulfilled, proud, and grateful.

I was part way there. I was shaking up my model of the world. No longer connecting the dots but starting with a blank canvas. It took some time to figure out what I wanted. It took more time still, to give permission to want it. I wanted to coach, I wanted to write, and I wanted to be a public speaker. The picture was becoming clearer, and part of me was excited. The other part wasn't sure. Who was I to be a coach? Who would want my advice? What kind of story did I have to tell? It wasn't all that exciting. What wisdom did I have to impart? I was still figuring things out. What was my value add?

I set very high expectations for myself. I'm the kind of person who sits my boss down to discuss how I have concerns about my own performance. Perfect was definitely the enemy of the good. I knew I was never going to be perfect, but dammit, I sure was going to try. I have a wonderfully loving and supportive family. The words I love you, good job, and I'm proud of you were never in short order. I never had to do anything but my best. And yet, I was constantly afraid of disappointing them.

In grade four, I was selected to be tested for an enrichment program. I remember little about the experience. I remember one question, and I remember that I got it wrong. I also remember the day I came home from school and found a note on my front door. It had been intended for my Dad, and it said, "She didn't get in." My first taste of failure and one I wouldn't forget. It later became a joke whenever I did something silly. Like the time a family friend convinced me there were left-handed and right-handed brooms. A chuckle, and throwaway comment, "That's my gifted child." It wasn't meant to be hurtful, but it was. We joked a lot in my family and this was one joke I couldn't take. It reminded me I had failed, and I felt like I wasn't good enough.

Over the years, I had a similar feeling whenever a B interrupted my straight A's. In grade eight I earned an academic A but not the athletic A. In high school I was on the honor roll four years but not five. I graduated university with honors, but as a guest at my graduation noted, not with distinction. The places I fell short seemed to negate the things I did well. They were all worthy achievements, and still I only heard the negative.

This applied to relationships as well. I made friends easily but best friends forever didn't seem to apply to me. As people grow, they sometimes grow apart, this was natural. And yet, I always thought I was to blame. Was there something wrong with me? Why did some people get to stay in the inner circle and I didn't? I was a good friend but not always one you kept around for the long haul.

I managed to make this pattern fit my romantic relationships as well. My parents divorced when I was quite young. I like to think it didn't impact me, but when it came to how I viewed relationships it definitely did. I don't think my Dad dated much after my mom, and if he did we didn't talk about it. My mom dated some, and was even remarried for a time. I wasn't the biggest fan of some of the men in her life. I didn't like seeing her get hurt. I often didn't have insight into what went wrong in these relationships, I just didn't like seeing her sad. I didn't want to be sad, and I definitely didn't want to be a divorcee. So, despite very much wanting to have a relationship I avoided them.

I guarded my heart and built up walls. Not so much with the intention of keeping people out but in an attempt to see who would climb them. There were a couple of times when I let my guard down, and put myself out there. Both times, when it didn't work out, I was quickly replaced by someone else. If I wasn't already comparing myself to other girls, I sure was now. In retrospect, I am able to look back at these situations with much greater perspective, but at the time, the message was loud and clear. I wasn't good enough.

As I reflect on this limiting belief, the idea I was never enough, I can see it's rather silly. I was being hypercritical. Intellectually I can provide context, explanation, and refute each one of these beliefs. And yet the feelings were very real for me, and therefore valid. They were also exhausting, and not getting me anywhere. An old roommate of mine had a notepad that said, 'put on your big girl panties and deal with it.' After all, as Karamo Brown says, "life does not happen to you, life responds to you." It was time I stopped feeling sorry for myself, stepped up and did something about it. I needed to be the leading lady in my own life, instead of settling for being the best friend.

Over the next few years, I made progress. Focusing and refocusing on how I wanted to feel rather than checking off boxes I thought needed to be checked. I started inching forward. I asked more questions, and made fewer assumptions. I began to replace criticism with curiosity. I acknowledged and celebrated my accomplishments. I started to feel myself realign with my authentic being. Things were good. At least they were until I would catch a glimpse of myself in the mirror. Who was that person?

I knew I had a weight problem, but when did it get this bad? How did this happen? I mean, I know how it happened but more importantly what happened? I didn't recognize myself. I didn't look like that in my head. What I was seeing on the outside didn't match who I thought I was on the inside.

I have always seen myself as overweight, and I suppose if you think something long enough, you start to believe it. I'm not suggesting I thought myself fat, that's not how it works. What I am saying, is that in many ways I manifested the weight. Created it to serve some sort of purpose. What that is, I'm not entirely sure. I have some suspicions, but the real reason, that one is buried deep and it would appear my unconscious mind isn't ready to talk about it just yet.

I don't know when I started eating my feelings, but I did. It was obviously easier than dealing with emotions I didn't seem to know how to process. I have experienced depression off and on since high school. My coping mechanisms were typically sleep and avoidance. Comfort food and TV eased the burden of being awake. Sometimes it just tasted good, and damn that sugar was addicting. Over time, it simply became habit.

In many ways, I think the weight became a form of protection. If boys weren't going to like me, it might as well be because I'm fat. That would be on them, right? They were too superficial to see the real me, and therefore it wasn't me they didn't like, it was my body. It was also a way of keeping me inside my comfort zone, as I didn't have the confidence to stray far. And I couldn't fail at things if I didn't bother to try anything new.

Shopping for clothes was a depressing nightmare that often ended in tears. Quick fix there - stop shopping. Just keep wearing the ol' standby that still fit. I mean, who doesn't love that huge sweatshirt from five years ago? Don't have something to wear? Don't go out. I became selective about who I spent time with. I stopped connecting with old friends. I simply couldn't be the girl who let herself go.

I even missed out on the funeral for my friend's mother, a woman I truly adored. How narcissistic is that? I mean, absolutely no one would be paying attention to me and yet, how I felt about my appearance was strong enough to blind me to the rest. One of the few regrets I have to this day. What the hell was I thinking?

I hated summer because it meant shorts and t-shirts. Worse still tank tops and bathing suits. I had always loved swimming, as a kid you could hardly keep me out of the water. Now I avoided it at all costs. You wouldn't catch this girl stripping down to a bathing suit. No, thank you! I had no desire to expose myself for all to see. Nor did I want to listen to my skinny friends talk about how they felt fat. If they were fat, what was I? It was easier to stay inside and enjoy the air conditioning. Bonus, I could probably get away with long sleeves.

I stopped having any active interests. I didn't want to do things where there was a chance I'd be out of breath. I avoided things where my weight or size might be highlighted. Flights or rides where seatbelts might not be big enough, canoeing where people would see how much I weighed down the boat, and of course anything with an actual weight limit. I often wondered if I'd be the one putting the elevator at capacity.

Being fat, feeling fat, and thinking fat managed to outweigh all the things I liked about myself. It was my ultimate shame. For me, it symbolized every failure, every mistake, and every way in which I didn't measure up. What must people think of me? I must be lazy, or lack self-control. How did I ever think I was going to influence people or be taken seriously looking like this? I had to find a way to let go of this weight.

Over the years I tried lots if things. Various diets and fitness regimes. Boot camps, group classes, personal training. Cleanses, fasting, you name it. It worked in fits and starts but nothing seemed to last. I felt stuck and I didn't know what to do. I was in a meeting once where we were trying to solve a problem. I do not remember the specifics, but I do remember feeling like we were banging our heads against a wall. My boss at the time posed a question I have never forgotten. She asked, "What would we never do?" I absolutely love this question and now ask it all the time. It is a great way to get a fresh perspective, to look at things from a completely different angle. It may not be the final answer, but it definitely gets the ideas flowing. So here, in this moment where I felt stuck. Where I was unsure what to do, I asked myself, "What would I never do?" The answer, CrossFit.

There are many ways to lose weight. Calories in, calories out and all that jazz. When it comes to the calories out portion of that equation, I would have chosen almost anything over CrossFit. I was bad at sports, and not in a cute way. A more accurate description would be athletically challenged. It looked intense, and not only hard, but impossible. It also seemed extremely competitive, and it's no fun competing for last place. I immediately had failure in my sights. Attempting CrossFit was essentially taking all my fears and limiting beliefs putting them into one experience and making me face them, all at once. I was afraid the real athletes would judge me, wondering what the fat girl was doing here and how was she going to keep up. I was worried I would never be able to do it, and that my value as a person was somehow tied to that. I was raised to be a strong and independent woman; there was no way I wanted to put my weaknesses out there for all to see. I had no desire to have anything to do with CrossFit, the Universe however, 'She' had other plans.

If you ask me, the Universe can be a bit of a low-talker. She starts with a faint whisper that often goes unnoticed. It comes again, and you may turn your head wondering if maybe you heard something. Next time you definitely know you heard something, but it was hard to decipher exactly what she said. You may get it the next time around though; have that moment where you stop and think, "Hmm, does this mean something?" And finally, when all her efforts have been ignored, the Universe smacks you in the face as if to say, "Can you hear me now?!" I don't know about you, but I tend to need to be smacked in the face.

The Universe had been planting this CrossFit seed for years. She planted a CrossFitter in my home and another down the street. I ignored them. A couple years later, she planted CrossFit gyms on route to yoga and the grocery store. I drove right on past. A year after that, CrossFit infiltrated my workplace, both domestic and international offices. These people were a little more persistent. This time I was a little more conscious in my health and fitness efforts and a colleague was certain CrossFit was the logical next step. He even went as far as to look up locations in my area. In my mind, I was still nowhere near ready for CrossFit. I, like so many others, was adamant I needed to be fit first. "2017," I said, "We'll talk about it in 2017." That put an end to that conversation, for the time being anyway. You see, the Universe may be a low-talker but she sure is a keen listener. By December 2016 she was in cahoots with that Zuckerberg kid, and my Facebook Newsfeed was plastered with it. CrossFit. Little to no experience. Women. Just six weeks. Insert ridiculously inspirational video here. Might as well have had my name written all over it. Well played Universe, well played.

CrossFit was nothing like I expected. Sure, it was hard. The struggle was definitely real, but it was doable. Everything could be modified, and every modification was building up to something else. It wasn't about trying to do the absolute hardest thing, but the next hardest thing. I expected the athletes to be intimidating, and full of themselves. That was definitely not the case. The community curated by the coaches was amazing. I loved how invested everyone was in the success of their fellow athletes. They genuinely rooted for each other and celebrated individual wins as a collective. They were a source of accountability, encouragement, and inspiration. Competition was less about winning and more about pushing ourselves further than we thought we could go. For the first time in my life I was okay coming in last, because I still won. I beat out my self-doubt and limiting beliefs. I gave 110% and for the first time in a long time, I had some confidence back.

Our coaches are all about helping us live our best lives, so it's no surprise the impact CrossFit has had both inside and outside the box. After all, how you do one thing is how you do everything. Old me, you remember her, she was the one lying on the floor in the depths of despair. Old me, she didn't get this phrase. She thought it meant if she failed at one thing, she would fail at everything. Well, with that attitude, she was probably right. I however, saw things a whole lot clearer.

The things that served me in CrossFit have organically started serving me in pursuit of all my goals. I now have coaches in other areas of my life – relationships, career, finances. If there was a coach for laundry, I'd sign up for that too! I've joined other communities of like-minded individuals working towards making their good lives, great lives. I have friends and colleagues who help keep me accountable. And instead of being intimidated by those who are ahead of me, I surround myself with them as an opportunity to learn and to grow. I even use the clock to help me get things done around the house. I set a timer and instead of how many reps can I do in 15 minutes, it's how many chores can I do. It may be taking things a bit far, but this girl is getting stuff done!

If I can approach all my goals, if I can approach life, the way I approach CrossFit, I can do anything. The box is the place where I feel challenged, exposed, uncomfortable, and exhausted. It is also the place where I've found it within myself to rise to the occasion, to be vulnerable, to be comfortable being uncomfortable, and to keep going when I don't think I have any more to give. It's where my independence gives way to interdependence.

And when everything else seems overwhelming, and I'm tempted to just lie down on the floor and cry, I go back to my one thing. I make sure I stay rooted in CrossFit. When I want to quit something, I go to the one place I refuse to quit. When I don't know how to do something, I come to a place where someone can give me guidance. When I don't know if I can do something I come to the place where I can see how far I've come. When I feel like I can't do it on my own, I come to a place where I don't have to. When I feel like I can't manage all the things, I just focus on this one thing because how I do that one thing, is how I do everything.

Erin Pellow lives Toronto, Ontario and is currently creating a life that lights her up! She is a success coach with Every Kind of Possible, supporting women as they transition from a good life, to a great life. In her spare time, she likes to paint, travel, and get lost in conversation. She also enjoys making puns and obscure pop culture references. While Erin dislikes burpeees, wall balls, thrusters, and lunges, she loves CrossFit. This winter she competed in her first CrossFit Games Open and this spring she embarks on her next challenge, training for her first 5k run.

I have accepted fear as a part of life –
specifically the fear of change....
I have gone ahead despite the pounding in the heart
that says: turn back.

~Erica Jong

Julie Steeves Benson

Removing the Mask

Growing up in a household where domestic violence unfortunately existed, was difficult and complex. My mother, my four siblings and I were all subjected to varying degrees of physical, mental, and emotional abuse.

The start of the violence for my mother was when she became pregnant out of wedlock. Back in those days it was really frowned upon to be pregnant and unmarried. You were thought of as promiscuous, or not a nice girl, unlike today where unmarried women are having babies with multiple partners and it seems to be more acceptable. My mother was two months pregnant when my parents exchanged vows. During my mother's pregnancy, my father beat her, punching her belly when she was months into the pregnancy with my older sister.

My sister was born in 1959, I was born in 1960, thirteen and half months later. What is incredulous to me, is that even with all the abuse that occurred, my parents continued to have more babies, increasing the financial stress of clothing and feeding five children.

Only our closest friends knew what was occurring in our household. It was kept pretty hush hush, friends comforted us when necessary. No one seemed to be able to do anything about it. The sad thing was the fact it was not unique in our middle-class neighborhood. As kids, we listened to each other's family stories but then would forget about them until the next time an event would occur. We thought it was part of being a family, the norm. We weren't happy about it but accepted it to some degree.

My parents seemed to cope less as we got older, my father became more volatile, my mother more robotic. This became more apparent as we developed and voiced our own opinions and as we started to understand the difference between what was right and wrong.

When some kids in our neighborhood heard about how my father was treating his girls, they dumped sugar in his gas tank. This caused havoc for me in particular. My father blamed my friends, insisting that I had put them up to it. I told him he was crazy. Not the smartest thing to say to someone who is hot-tempered. No amount of explaining would save me. I was telling the truth, but he simply did not believe me. I became the black sheep in my family, the trouble maker for speaking out, defending myself. Which looking back seemed so ridiculous. Standing up for what was right, what was truthful was unfortunately not a good idea.

I tried calling the police during one incident when my father was on a tirade. I felt my siblings were in danger. He clubbed me across the side of my face when he caught me dialing the phone. I passed out, falling and taking a dish rack full of dishes with me. I tried calling the police again when I came to. He then grabbed the phone from my hand and smashed my wrist with it, giving me a hairline fracture. The police came but it was all swept under the carpet, dismissed. I felt destroyed. He was such a sweet talker. "You know kids they are so dramatic."

I ended up in the hospital having jaw surgery for a displaced mandible. During recovery and while still under the effects of the anaesthetic, I was apparently questioned about the accident, groggily I told them my father had hit me. When I did get released from the hospital, I ended up telling everyone else that the injury was caused from falling off a horse. It seemed easier to cover up the truth than have to withstand more questions. I did feel like the adults never believed the kids, and if they did believe us, they did not want to get involved.

The abuse was intermittent but had occurred enough times that my grandmother, who knew how her son was, offered to help my mother move us all out of harms way. My mother was too afraid to do so. The thought of taking care of five children on her own, in another town or city was too daunting and financially long term it seemed for her a pending nightmare. She stayed, so we had to stay.

I constantly worried about our safety. I was a worry wart of a kid. It was like living on eggshells daily, never knowing what mood my father might be in when he came home from work. Wondering what might trigger him to pop a blood vessel and go nuts on us, my mother included. We grew to know the signs of an impending assault, the bulging eyes, the purple face, the clenched fists and threatening words. Depending upon the circumstances my mother would try to protect us. Sometimes my mother would be able to give us a heads up, warn us that dad was in a bad mood.

He also had a cruel streak. His idea of teaching life skills was questionable at the best of times. To teach me how hot the furnace could get, he took my hand and placed it on the hottest part of the furnace, until my hand blistered and I screamed.

Teaching us about nature was very tricky too. Once he sent me into a pitch black, musty smelling cave. I crawled carefully on my belly until he told me to stop. I wasn't to turn the flashlight on until he said so. He hollered at me to lay on my back and shine the light to the ceiling of the low hanging cave. I screamed as soon as I turned the flashlight on. There were hundreds of spiders and their sacks full of baby spiders hanging within inches of my face. I was petrified! He said I needed to be "toughened up."

I wondered about his past, his time in the military, and his own childhood. Why did he think I needed toughening up? My older sister got the brunt of it. She was the first born and the disappointment. My father had wanted a boy. She was subjected to a lot of name calling and physical abuse, to toughen her up. It didn't 'toughen us up' as much as it 'fucked us up.'

We found out from my grandmother that my father had split his head open as a child and he was never the same after that. I don't know if that was an excuse, an attempt to justify or perhaps just to hide his personality flaws.

Once he punished me because I could not pronounce or sound out the word 'tube'. I had never seen that word before and have never forgotten it since. He forced me to sit in the dark in our scary basement until I did figure it out, hours passed. I sat at the top of the basement stairs as the furnace made such a terrifying noise; my knees tucked into my chest, shivering and scared. My older sister was on the other side of the door trying to console me. I was in first grade at the time.

He always seemed to test us, see if we could outrun him, or be stronger than him. He knew we couldn't compete with him, but he pushed us anyway, which regularly became an opportunity for him to put us down, and ultimately make him feel powerful.

Christmas could be a painful time, as he would choose one sibling and blatantly spoil them. He was mean that way. We would never know why we didn't measure up that particular year. We just accepted it, never daring to say anything. It caused jealousies and hurt feelings among my sisters and I.

He would spoil my mother which made us all happy. He would put a number on each gift he gave her and she would count them out. One year she received thirty gifts. To me it was a strange game. My mother was the happiest on Christmas Day. I always thought he was trying to make up for all the bad things he did. After the holidays, he would complain bitterly about the cost of Christmas and the bills that piled up because of it. January and February were never great months in our household. Heads would roll easily. It was very confusing for me.

If I needed dental work or books for school, I had to pay for them from my babysitting money. I didn't go to the dentist for many years. All my father's spare money would be spent on his hiking gear, expensive climbing ropes and cameras. Never on things we kids needed like shoes or clothes.

My mother worked part-time. She did her best to help with our basic needs, bless her, but her hands were tied. She never had a say in what he purchased. He was the breadwinner and that made him happy which was a positive thing. My father did not want my mother to work full-time. He wanted dinner on the table when he got home. He had everything under control except his temper.

I know he cared for us in his way because he would have emergency fire drills in the dead of winter, in the middle of the night. We would have to escape in our pyjamas into the freezing cold air and sometimes drop out of a window into his arms. He never let us fall to the ground. He was a man of extremes.

It was often unnerving. This same man who would take us for ice cream, teach us to appreciate the outdoors, take us to a local park to run around and spend hours with us tobogganing, was the same man who would threaten to throw us off a cliff if we misbehaved. The same man who would lock us in a dark basement for hours, punch us, back hand us and whip us with a coat hanger.

Once in a while my mother was brave enough to stand up to him. One time she was belaying my dad on a ninety-foot cliff. He was swearing at her because she didn't have the tension right with the rope. He was getting angrier and angrier, calling her names. My sisters and I were standing near her looking up praying this would all be over soon, but kind of half hoping that he would be stuck dangling on the side of the cliff forever. My mother who was fairly quiet finally had enough, when he swore at her one more time, she yelled back telling him that she would drop him if he didn't stop swearing at her. In his infinite wisdom he swore at her one more time. With a serious look on her face she told us to run. She looked up at my dad then let go of the rope. He fell over twenty feet into the mud below. He was so angry he couldn't speak. He may have had the wind knocked out of him. We laughed nervously from a distance but not within his hearing range. He never said a word to my mother. She never helped him again with his cliff climbing because I am pretty sure he never asked her to.

Hearing "you're worthless", "you will never amount to anything", "you're a deadbeat" had a huge impact on me. I suffered with confidence and trust issues for years. When I look back now it was pretty messed up. The fall out was, as I gained traction in my life and entered counseling, I decided to prove my father wrong.

From a young age, I knew I would have to survive on my own. This was impressed upon me at regular intervals in my teenage years by my parents who encouraged us to leave home permanently as early as possible.

There was never talk or encouragement regarding post high school education or career choices. The thought of leaving home was becoming very appealing yet also scary. I was thinking about it more and more.

Somewhere along the way I started praying in vain. I wanted the madness to stop, the bullying, the breaking of bones and the insults. I hated what it was doing to my sisters and to my mother. Each of us was suffering in our own way.

A painful memory of my older sister being strangled, the blood running down her face is an image that will be etched in my mind forever. Once you see it, you can't unsee it. My sister and my dad were arguing, I heard her cries from the main floor of our home and ran upstairs as I knew it would not be a good scene. I wanted to rescue her, but I froze when I saw him with his eyes bulging, his one hand around her neck, his other hand in a fist. Her face was all bloody. I cried out and ran as fast as I could to get help, screaming through the neighborhood looking for my mother. I thought my dad was going to kill my sister. I was terrified.

I don't know where my other siblings were during the attack. It felt like everything was moving in slow motion. I did find my mother, having tea with a neighbor, I bawled that dad was going to kill my sister. The neighbor started freaking out and I never saw my mother move so fast.

The result was we were all removed from our home by the court. We went to live with our aunt, who wasn't our real aunt by blood, but was a very close friend of my father's mother. She knew the nitty-gritty on my dad and took us in right away.

My sisters and I had to travel almost two hours, taking two buses and a subway to get from my aunt's apartment in the center of Toronto to our suburban elementary school. Sometimes it felt like an adventure, taking care of my three younger sisters. None of us could really grasp what was going on, except that dad had done something really bad this time, and we couldn't live at home.

Our aunt was wonderful. We loved her cool apartment and she made us feel special. It was quiet, peaceful and most importantly I felt safe. I hoped my sisters did too.

The court eventually allowed us to move back home. I was giddy with excitement. I truly believed that we would live happily ever after.

To my sister's horror once we were back at home, my mother made her apologize to my father. For provoking him to beat the crap out of her and then having to go to court.

My father had convinced my mother that things would be good moving forward. My sister's relationship with my mother changed forever that day. The betrayal weighed heavily on my sister. My mother did it because my dad insisted on an apology, which my sister had no choice but to begrudgingly give him. My mother did not want to raise us on her own.

Stressed from the abuse at home and sleeping with a knife under my pillow occasionally, I was always on edge. I tried to commit suicide at thirteen because I really believed I was worthless. I didn't really know how to actually commit suicide, so it was a bit of a debacle. It was however a cry for help. The psychologist found nothing much wrong with me which was a bigger surprise to me than my parents. It was suggested that my parents attend counseling, but that went over like a lead balloon. I was punished and sent away for a month to my grandparents, which wasn't much of a punishment.

At fifteen I visited my family doctor who suggested I leave home and organized the paperwork for me. I remember his words clearly "You have to take care of yourself before you can take care of anyone else." My mother, bless her, didn't blink an eye when I gave her the documents that would make me ward of the court. She seemed like a robot at the time. In retrospect

I now know she was just a shell of a woman. I was one less mouth to feed. One less stressor. I endured high school living on student welfare. I felt all alone, but always had faith that I would figure life out. I was so worried about my mother and my siblings, that I couldn't eat without getting sick myself. That was the first time I learned about ulcers.

When I felt strong, I would visit my family. On one visit my father noticed my weight loss. He always commented on our weight or our appearance. He hugged me tight and seemed so glad to see me. It was nice to see him, or so I thought, until he grabbed my face and tried to shove his tongue in my mouth. I was horrified, repulsed and shoved him back. Even writing about it makes me want to vomit. Tears come like the roar of a waterfall thinking back to what I endured. I can't forget the smug look on his face.

This was the same father, who tried to get me to watch the Baby Blue movies with him and was very disappointed when I wouldn't. I knew what those movies were about as I had discovered them accidentally while babysitting late one night at a neighbors. I muddled through my teenage years, working on creating healthy boundaries with my family.

Many years before my father passed away, we made amends at his father's funeral; which was cathartic on many levels. Forgiveness and compassion were so important in moving forward in my life. I thought everyone deserved a second chance.

In my forties I thought domestic violence was far behind me, couldn't touch me again, but it reared its ugly head. I avoided dating for many years after my amicable divorce. I thought joining a monastery would be easier than dating but those thoughts were fleeting, and I was not Catholic. When I did date, I was super cautious. I didn't want to subject my daughter to men I thought wouldn't be there for the long haul. I was super protective.

Then a man that I met on a plane wooed me for weeks on end. He wrote beautiful poetry in his emails. We had made what I thought was a spiritual connection. He happened to be in the same city I was traveling to for business. I mentioned where I was staying and that we could meet up for coffee or dinner. There was a knock at my hotel door, I was surprised by how he knew my room number as I had not given it to him. I unlocked the door anyway. It all happened so fast and with such force. I tried to fight him off, but he was very aggressive. He sexually assaulted me.

I was scared and confused by what had taken place. I boarded the airplane that weekend to return home. Sunglasses covering my bloodshot eyes from crying into the wee hours. I never reported what happened, because I was fearful of the ramifications of doing so. The police couldn't help when I was a kid so why would they help me now. I had heard so many women in the news saying how they were judged when they reported they were raped that I decided not to say anything. I thought by not reporting it, it would disappear like a bad dream.

Of course, it didn't. It haunted me regularly. I berated myself, questioning how I ever got into that situation in the first place. It really messed with my head. Would they think I asked for it to happen? I didn't want to be judged. I felt too vulnerable to expose myself to the judicial process and worse, my family and friends.

Fast forward ten years or more to my daughter moving back home, eight months pregnant. I was mortified to find out that she had been experiencing abuse in her relationship. It was the third time she had left someone because of their nasty behavior. Part of me couldn't believe that my daughter would ever have to endure domestic violence. I felt like I had let her down somehow, had been unable to protect her.

196

My daughter gave birth to a beautiful baby girl, making me a grandmother for the first time. A role I cherished. I realized I was going to have to go to an uncomfortable place and tell my daughter she had to report the abuse to her doctor. I put the incredible shame I carried aside and told her about what happened to me in the hotel room, by someone I thought I knew. What daughter wants to hear that their mom has been sexually assaulted? It was a moment of truth, and relief. I needed my daughter to understand that verbal, physical and emotional abuse should never be acceptable, ever. I am grateful she took my advice.

I realized at this juncture in my life that I had to do more about domestic issues. I thought about my granddaughter, growing up in a society where she might encounter these matters. It made me want to stand at a pulpit and yell to anyone who would listen that our society needs to change. I knew I had to take a more active role somehow in helping facilitate these societal issues. I started volunteering on the board of My Friend's House, a shelter for abused women and their children.

I also contributed a story for one of their spring newsletters. I used my initials, not my full name, because I was nervous at what the reaction would be if someone read it and knew it was me... I was paranoid.

A Very Personal Story

"My mother had experienced domestic abuse for years. I was in my 30's when I encouraged my mother to leave her husband, my father. My parents had moved to a rural farmhouse in the country. My mother was isolated and cut off from her daughters and friends. She didn't drive and there were no buses. I was very conflicted as I knew how timid and afraid my mother was to leave him.

She had thought about it many times over the years, but financially she believed she couldn't do it. Emotionally she was so broken she literally had no self-esteem left. She was depressed and fearful; as I had been as a teenager.

I had grown up witnessing and experience my father's abuse. Fractured bones, bruises, 911 calls, strangulation, inappropriate behavior, belittlement, whippings and burns. Domestic abuse in the 60's and 70's was not talked about and was usually swept under the carpet. There was a real stigma for women with children, let alone a woman with five.

At fifteen I left home. With counseling I survived it and realized I did have value, I was worth something. I wanted my mother to feel and experience that too. I told her about a woman's shelter that could help.

To leave was the toughest thing my mother ever did, and the bravest. She left the comfort of a relationship, married for a long time. I was proud of her. She grew up in an era where leaving wasn't an option.

A woman's shelter is where my mother received counseling, hope, and support. It took time for my mother to enjoy her new life. She had many struggles with depression, but she experienced freedom for the first time in decades living without fear. My mother passed away in 2000 of lung cancer, in my fortieth year.

I am deeply grateful in my heart and soul for how she did her best with what she had. She was such a humble woman. I am a volunteer with My Friend's House so I know the positive impact that women's shelters provide. This tribute is in honor of my mother, my friend. She was the one who inspired me to never give up and always be kind and compassionate."

Despite all the things that I have been through in my life, I will continue to hold my head up high, because I was meant to thrive not just survive.

Feeling brave one day I revealed to a few friends that I had written the story. They were shocked. Comments included, "I would have never known." "You don't appear like you were abused." It was very freeing in many ways to confess to them because the truth is, we don't know what abuse looks like. It doesn't have an age, skin color, religion or a gender to discern itself. We don't know what is going on behind closed doors... or behind the eyes of a friend or even a stranger. Until the mask is removed.

Julie Steeves Benson is an author born in Ontario, Canada. She is a human rights champion, video writer and developer, as well as an avid hiker. In her spare time founded and manages AOK, Ambassador of Kindness to help inspire kindness. F*ck Fear is her debut as a contributing author to The Sisterhood Folios. Julie has also written Lonely Kings and Queens, a sensual book of poetry.

You gain strength, courage, and confidence by every experience in which you really stop to look fear in the face.
You are able to say to yourself, 'I lived through this horror. I can take the next thing that comes along.'

~Eleanor Roosevelt

Mia Valente

Sexy, Fearless and Fierce

What does it mean to be sexy, fearless and fierce? I surely didn't have the answer at 21 years old. I didn't discover it until I was 27. To help you understand, I will have to take you back to the beginning.

I knew he would be a significant part of my life when we first met on that hot August day outside of the Soulpepper Theatre Co. in Toronto. It was the summer of 2007, I just turned seventeen. I was hanging out with my 'Mija,' she is still one of my best friends today and she introduced us. I instantly felt an attraction to him, he intrigued me. As life would have it, I was already in a relationship, so I didn't act on these feelings. We became friends and remained in touch

The relationship I was in ended on good terms over the Christmas break of 2007. By early 2008, I was single and in the Youth Leadership Program at Soulpepper. He was also in this program. We just started hanging out together, in and outside of the group. I really grew to like him as time went on. In May we went on our first real date. He asked me to go to the movies with his friends, but when I got there it was just him. Later he admitted he used his friends as cover because he was too shy to ask me out. Pretty much the next couple months were filled with shameless flirting and while that was happening, I started falling hard and fast for him.

The summer of 2008 we spent as much time as we could with each other. We were just teens in love, hanging out, swimming and exploring our city. One of my favorite memories is from the day we spent at the beach. Watching his face while I stripped down to my bikini and then asked him to rub lotion on my back. It was that kind of teasing love.

It was one of the best summers of my life. I was truly happy! I had amazing friends, who are still in my life to this day and an amazing boyfriend. I also got accepted into college. I knew it would remain real even after the summer, we were totally in love. I really cared about him so much. We were always talking about the future and we discovered we wanted the same things. I wanted it all with him, to be his wife, have his children and to build a life together. It was a childhood dream of mine to find the love of my life. I remember I spent days by the bay as a child daydreaming about it. I had finally found true love and never wanted to let it go.

As a child, I was always very intuitive, loving, sensitive and kind of shy. I had friends, but I remember spending time alone deep in my thoughts by the bay. I could read situations around me pretty well and was usually right on. My mother used to say that my head was always in the clouds.

I had for the most part a happy childhood. Of course there were tough times, ups and downs and hardships also. But overall I had two parents that in their own way tried hard to raise me the best they could and later at age nine, I gained two more parents. Together, the four of them, along with my grandparents raised and instilled in me the values and morals that I still have today. By my late teens as an overall happy child, I had close relationships with my step-sibling, all four parents, cousins and amazing friends.

By May 2010, he and I were together for 2 years. Our relationship was way past the honeymoon phase, but the love was still there.

He would leave me love notes, we would cook together and we traveled. I was so in love. It was such a pure unconditional love that I became blind to the signs that something was not quite right.

It started subtly, he would get angry at me for silly reasons and it would turn into intense rage. I couldn't understand it. It ranged from not giving him the right advice when he ask me for it, to wearing shoes that did not make sense in his eyes. In hindsight, it would have been best to leave then, however I was in love. I wanted to work it out and support him.

We were in the underground heading home, after a date one night, when he started telling me weird things like "I know how to manipulate people." About a month later, he told me about the time, as a pre-teen, he hurt someone on purpose, out of anger and they ended up in the hospital. I didn't think anything of it at the time.

By the end of 2010, the relationship had gone downhill. The criticism was becoming stronger, every time we were together I did something wrong. Then I would defend myself and he would apologize. The next time we were together this was repeated. I heard how I couldn't take care of myself because I wore stupid shoes, how I wasn't what he wanted, that he didn't want to get married or have kids. Then the next day, he wanted it all with me.

I remember going out drinking with my girlfriends. If a guy showed any interest in me I thought about running away with them and forgetting about the love of my life. I learned that this was probably the time my subconscious knew something was truly wrong. I was so hurt. I did not do anything about it, but I was tempted.

I felt like I was on a rollercoaster. He was doing and saying hurtful things and then apologizing saying "I am so in love with you!"

I figured he was struggling and I was there to support him. So I stayed.

I was losing myself in the relationship, so I made a point to get reconnected with my friends before it was too late and never lose them again. That decision was the best one I ever made. By now it was May 2011.

I also started doing things independently which made me feel better and started dressing more like myself again. I was looking and felt good at 21 years old. But the issues with my relationship continued. Where was the love? There was a nagging feeling in my gut telling me *Emilia leave, you are in an abusive relationship*. I ignored it, thinking there was no indication of abuse, we are only fighting. I chalked it up to fear and would not be overcome by it.

Then came that night, when I realized maybe my inner voice was right. I remember the moment, it was right after we had sex. He gave me a very hard slap when I wasn't looking. I was so angry! I yelled at him, told him to never do that again. He kept hitting me until I yelled back loudly to stop. He did, but then he started to laugh and said "I wanted to see the marks it would leave, relax Em. I will never do that again."

I told him he needed to go to therapy or else I was done. He agreed, apologized and it didn't happen again until a few weeks later. Then again and again. Each time he apologized and blamed his depression.

I was very confused, in my head I figured out this was abuse, but I still had doubts because it had only been a couple of isolated incidents. If it's inconsistent, is it really abuse? Yes! Inconsistent abuse is still abuse and the more you ignore it, the more consistent it can become.

I really had no clue at 21 years of age, about how abusive people operate. The abuse escalated the more I asserted my boundaries. But I didn't leave.

One day I found myself pinned down on a bed and he spit on me. It happened out of nowhere and was really upsetting. I tried standing up but he pushed me back down hard. He was laughing as he was doing this. I remember breaking free, spitting back and hitting him in self-defense. He got so angry at me for disrespecting him. I cried that night. I was so confused, yet I couldn't just leave him. He always apologized and said he didn't understand what was going on in his head.

I was so torn, I wanted to help him battle his demons, but at what cost? I forgave him again, hoping that would be the last incident. It was not. A couple of weeks later, a scarier moment happened, one that years later I realized could be considered sexual assault. I remember his hands around my neck during sex, him laughing down at my face saying "It's fucking like I am raping you!" I was shaken to the core. I yelled at him but I should have left.

He used his mental health issues as an excuse again. We booked a therapy appointment, a condition that I demanded if I was going to stay. We also had a trip to England coming up that was non-refundable. I wasn't sure how to leave or what to do. I was feeling scared, embarrassed and I felt like no one would believe me. Here I was a confident young lady and I was allowing him to do this, for what? Love? I was pretty sure healthy love was not this. He would always apologize but I kept hearing my mama's voice "Em, you don't have to keep going through this." I wasn't listening. I didn't want give up on us. I wanted to go back to 18 years old and feel that love again.

The weeks leading up to England, things calmed down and once there, things felt almost normal. He was kind of back to his old self, but we were still fighting and he was still saying cruel things at times. I thought, "Right, we will sort out his mental health, then work on rebuilding us." I was committed to him for the long term.

He asked me out to a Soulpepper performance when we returned to Canada. I felt things were getting better. I told him as soon as I confirmed that I could get the evening off from work, I would let him know about the performance. He said he would wait for my answer.

Well, I did get the evening off. I told him about three nights prior to when we were supposed to go, while I was over at his place. When I told him, he stopped me and told me that he was going with someone else, because I took too long to respond. I asked him to tell me who he was going with since he was supposed to be working on repairing us. He wouldn't tell me who but hinted it was another girl. I flipped on him. His response to my anger was "What? You're not my wife or my mom, you don't need to know." I responded "No asshole, I am your girlfriend of three and a half years." He turned on me saying I have trust issues. I told him "Fuck off."

I was about to go home but he told me not to make a scene because we had dinner with his family planned. I did not give two fucks at this point. I started putting on my jacket. He stopped me as I was opening the door to leave the condo, his tears threatening to spill and he said "I made this up, so I could get a true reaction out of you and now this proves to me you have trust issues." I was angry. He was playing mind games. This is not what I deserved.

I would later learn that what he did that October night was called gaslighting. I felt so violated, but still I stayed for dinner and went to the movies. The deciding factor was that evening, I realized I just had enough. The next day I planned to break it off with him. I wanted one last nice night with the him. But once again, he apologized and things were suddenly good. I asserted my boundaries again to him, saying that under no circumstances would this happen again. That he needed to ask me things directly, with no manipulation.

Later, after a peaceful dinner, we made our way over to the movie theatre. We were sitting at a table in the waiting area with our drinks when all of the sudden he grabbed my wrist hard and twisted it. "I am still so fucking pissed with you." I knew right then I was clearly in danger. I broke free and ran away crying, he laughed and said "What are you fucking going to do Em, cry?"

I walked away with my bag to the washroom. I stood in the mirror, my mascara running and said "This is not me; I am not this girl." I heard a voice in my head saying "Leave safely. Don't let him know your plans, stay and be safe. It's not safe to just leave him."

I watched the movie and kissed him goodbye. The next day we meet in a local coffee shop. I broke it off. I was done, he cried. I later learned this was a manipulation tactic, I felt horrible, but it had to be done. I asked for space, he wouldn't let up. I was being messaged all the time and he was confessing his unrelenting love for me.

I was confused because a part of me wanted to believe him. I was determined to find out his true intentions and to gather proof of his abusive behavior. I would not to be played, I was no fool. I was a beautiful, loving, caring woman. A friend told me to keep setting boundaries that put my interest first, you are standing your ground and manipulators hate that and will accuse you of trying to manipulate them and play the victim.

I swallowed my fear. I took him back with a hidden intention. I manipulated the manipulator to break free from this hold he had on me and to get the proof that I knew I needed.

My final thought was *Not today, motherfucker, you will never control me*. Let's just say this worked. Two weeks later I wrote "I'm done." It worked. No more second chances.He wrote this to me 'I think it's best we stop hanging out until you're ready to. Call me when you want, I'll leave you alone from now on. I feel the more I try to connect with you the more you respond in a way that disappoints me, the less I care and that's not good. So to reiterate, don't ask to hang out with me unless you're willing to give it your all and want to be around me and you don't have to worry about me contacting you too much." He also accused me of trying to manipulate him the night in a heated skype conversation before he wrote this email.

I felt free and empowered. I walked away and I could finally look forward. I wanted to move to London, start fresh. I was feeling pretty good. I wish I had known more about leaving abusive relationships. I didn't realize how angry he was. He kept calling that day I wrote "Done." It was November 5, 2011. I had forty missed calls. Many texts, demanding I talk to him. Then came the voicemail from him threatening to do something to himself or me. It was the only voicemail he left.

I called his brother to get him to a hospital, explaining that I broken up with him. I didn't want him hurt. While I was on the phone, I heard pounding on the front door. He was at my house. His eyes were dead with no emotion. I remembered the threatening message. I knew if I opened that door, I'd be dead.

I called 911, and his brother, telling him to come get him. His brother hummed and was stalling so I said "He is abusing me and I have called the cops!" I screamed and hung up and called 911 again and yelled at them to hurry up. I was terrified! Who the fuck was this monster? It lasted for 20 minutes, I was shaken up.

I walked out of the washroom and yelled at him to "Leave me alone" and "Get off my property." He eventually left, and I realized he knew everything about my house even where spare keys were. The police showed up, I showed the female cop the email. I had kept it, something in my inner voice had told me to. I played the voicemail also. They warned him.

He did not come around again but proceeded to cyber stalk me for months and was continuously contacting me, my family and friends. I was getting anonymous nasty letters in the mail. I was living in fear, I was staying at my friend's apartment for days, could not sleep in my own bed.

As months and days went by, the flashbacks and panic attacks were almost daily. I had to put on my brave face. I remember feeling alone, but I was handling and hiding it. I was applying for a work visa. I was hurting. I remember my mentor telling me on the phone, to think that I was 'fearless, sexy and fierce.' I rearranged it and that became my mantra.

Even if I didn't believe it, I would say it, I had no clue what it meant really, it just resonated with me. I was an emotional roller coaster between the six months after break up and before the illness manifested. Eventually it caught up with me, it become so intense that I didn't sleep properly for 5 days and I developed hallucinations.

My body cracked and I was later diagnosed with a serious chronic mental illness. The hallucinations were one thing, but the panic attacks, flashbacks and lack of sleep were always around. The emotions from abuse and the incident always around. I was always on flight or fight mode.

I now had mental illness to deal with and already faced some harsh stigma. I was afraid I was going to lose my friends, it had already damaged my relationship with some of my closest family members. There was so much fear. I hid my feelings of fear... from becoming ill again to being in another abusive relationship.

I didn't want to burden anyone. My emotions were so strong the first couple of years. I kept being transported to the day I thought I was going to be killed. Day in and day out, any stressful event or any person that reminded me of him would bring out the fight or flight emotions. I was always on edge. It became so intense, I still couldn't handle it two years after the break up.

In December 2013, I was facing a particularly stressful situation and battling these intense emotions again. I decided I would rather be dead then to go through this again and again. So, I did it. I took many pills, after begging for help at a local hospital and being turned away. I felt hopeless, I let his darkness become mine. I was not worth it, I was a failure, I was used goods, he was right. Everyone loved him, not me.

I was in so much internal pain, the intensity of emotions so strong. I wanted to leave, finish off what he was going to do that night, be out of this hell. But I always had a voice in my head saying "You aren't meant to die now, keep going."

I was living overseas at the time. I woke up in the ICU and then in a regular ward. I was disappointed because I had not died, but did not tell anyone. I felt like I would never be able to get over this. I was so angry, at him, God, everyone. But I never expressed it.

Developing a mental illness so young showed me how cruel we all are to individuals who suffer from mental illness. We really are. Yet the inner strength that got me to leave, would always come back and say "No, not your time, you are sexy, fearless and fierce." My intuition was strong. With the encouragement of my loved ones, each time I fell I got back up. This became a pattern.

By now, the stalking had stopped. He was apologizing and admitting the abuse. When I was 25 I was in my apartment, seeing someone when my intuition said to get over the fear and face it. So, I contacted my ex-boyfriend via email and said "I forgive you."

Once I sent that we ended up emailing each other. He was really apologizing. I wasn't sure if he telling the truth and eventually we met up in public place. I never stopped loving him, I will always love him, but I never again wanted to be with him or have him in my life. I didn't want to ruin his life. If I did I would have pressed harassment charges.

We met for a coffee, and found myself facing the man who I had become terrified of. It was strangely okay. To quote Beyoncé 'My torturer became my remedy.'

We talked on and off for a year. In that time, he admitted to the abuse he mentioned in the emails. He apologized truthfully and admitted that on the night he was angry he was going to hurt me.

It was the realest conversation we had together. The fear of him disappeared. There was nothing to fear, because I had already faced him and won when I left. When I moved overseas and dated again. There was no reason for me to be afraid of him. I tricked him and escaped, he seemed to be dealing with anger.

The best thing I did was leave. In his own words, "I am proud of you for standing up to your abusive boyfriend." I told my abuser that he had no chance to ever do those things to me again, that I was happy. That even after all this I wanted him to treat his next girlfriend right. That I loved him but I was glad I had left.

See my love was unconditional but my trust and respect were not. I told him we would have been together if he had not turned abusive and dealt with his anger.

I was so madly in love with him, I gave up everything to be with him. I wished him well. I truly understand his pain, it not an excuse, but I felt compassion for him. Hurt people sometimes hurt others. I cut communication for good October 2016, happy we came to an understanding and closure. It was liberating.

To my ex-boyfriend, "I wish you all the happiness that we both deserve. That you never hurt another person again and that you come to find peace within yourself. I will continue doing me and I am ready for my next stage in life. Thank you for teaching me my greatest life lesson, I am worth it."

Then the healing began, I could finally let it all go. By 2017 I was feeling better. Now I only look back on everything with gratitude.

Then, I finally figured out that I was being sexy, fearless and fierce the entire time. I was accessing my inner strength all long and getting up after each fall. I had been so constricted by fear and negativity, I had an incorrect perception of my life. I am truly a sexy, fearless and fierce woman.

My experience is what is driving my passion for social work. I want to give back and be a source of comfort and protection to those in need. Coming to the realization that I had experienced sexual assault, physical and emotional abuse really shook me to the core. It happened in waves, and took years to process. I understand what it's like to have experienced all three types of abuse, suffer from a mental illness and have intense compassion for those suffering.

If I can help just one person discover and use their inner strength to heal, that would make me happy. We all have inner strength and should feel worthy of love and care.

The world is both beautiful and cruel and I promise to make sure as long as I live to try and make it brighter. I am so grateful for everything that has happened, it has made me stronger. To the supportive friends and family for picking up in the moments I could not... thank you. My story is far from over and I am looking forward to experiencing it... as a sexy, fearless and fierce woman.

Born on the shores of Georgian Bay in July 1990, **Emilia (Mia) Valente** grew up in her early years in the small town of Parry Sound eventually settling in Toronto at age 8 with her family. Emilia graduated from George Brown College in 2011. A couple years later she moved and work overseas in London, England for a year-and-half. Upon her return, went back to school to for social work part-time.

Emilia enjoys writing and writes poetry as well her blog Sexy, Fearless Fierce. Emilia is also a big advocate for mental health and enjoys traveling, swimming, singing and spending time with love ones.

Each of us must confront our own fears, must come face to face with them. How we handle our fears will determine where we go with the rest of our lives. To experience adventure or to be limited by the fear of it.

-Judy Blume

Fear of Faltering

It was the beginning of what I thought was going to be the best year of my life. Grade 12. We were going on a class trip to Louisiana in April, and I was graduating in May. Life was good. I had a lot of friends, a cute boyfriend who drove a hot car and a busy social life.

It was a beautiful fall day on the prairies. A fellow classmate was celebrating her 18th birthday. My boyfriend at the time was away working, so I was going with Lyle and Bryan, a couple of our buddies. We were meeting up with some friends there. Lyle, Bryan and I had a few drinks before heading to the party. No teenage boy wants to leave his vehicle behind so we drove to the party four houses away. After hanging out at the party for a while we decided to go for a booze cruise.

Booze cruises are a common occurrence in the country. I grabbed my case of beer and away we went. I hopped into my friend's truck which had only two bucket seats. Since there were three of us I scooched to the middle and sat on a toolbox. I looked for my seatbelt but of course there wasn't one... I was sitting on a toolbox. I made sure the boys put their belts on before we left town. They complied but not without putting up a bit of a fuss. My whole life I was adamant about people wearing their seatbelts and I was always afraid of car accidents.

We headed out of town, music cranked, laughing and joking. Most people booze cruise around 30 kilometers per hour. We were going highway speed, about 90 to 100 kilometers per hour. It was just before midnight, so it was pitch black outside when all of a sudden there was a really sharp turn in the road. There was no sign marking the curve so it came up on us quickly. We were going too fast to turn in time. I remember thinking "we are going to roll" but I was surprisingly calm. I didn't feel fear, perhaps the alcohol I had consumed played a role in that. We just kept going straight off the road.

The truck rolled, many times, both end over and sideways. With no seatbelt holding me, I was thrown through the windshield. The truck, with my friends inside, kept rolling.

I remember waking up on grass, not able to see anything because of the darkness of the night, for a moment not understanding why I was there. I heard Lyle calling my name, looking for me, and then he found me. I got up and tried to walk, but I couldn't, I kept falling. I felt like I was stepping in gopher holes. Lyle picked me up and carried me to the truck.

Bryan was unconscious. He looked dead. I remember screaming his name over and over telling him "please don't die". Shock had set in and I felt no pain. Lyle noticed a set of car lights coming in our direction. I stayed with Bryan while Lyle ran out onto the road to get help. It turned out to be a classmate of mine Devon, who was on his way home from the party. Lyle picked me up and carried me to his vehicle. The interior light of the truck was on and I caught a glimpse of my face which was full of blood. The only thing I could see were the whites of my eyes.

Devon called his parents for help as they were less than a mile away. Then I called my parents and they called an ambulance. My older brothers set off to find us, while my mom stayed on the phone with me. I told her my face was full of blood and something was wrong with my leg. When I exclaimed I could see a light coming, my poor mom wasn't sure if I was seeing 'the light' or what exactly I was seeing.

The lights turned out to be one of my brothers and my brother-in-law. My brother picked me up and put me in my parent's car. As he carried me, my foot was dangling. I still felt no pain. My other brother, my dad, my sister and some friends were also at the scene by this time and they rushed to the truck where Bryan was still unconscious.

My dad, my sister and sister-in-law started driving me to meet the ambulance. By this time the shock was wearing off and I was starting to feel pain. I was scared and unsure of my injuries; I didn't know if I was going to die. I was also worried about Bryan, who was still out at the accident scene, trapped in the truck.

When we arrived at the hospital in Saskatoon, it was evident that I needed emergency surgery. The doctors decided to wait until the other two from the accident arrived at the hospital just in case one of them needed surgery more than I did. My foot was laying on the stretcher beside me but it was still attached to me by the ligaments and tendons.

The staff at the hospital treated me horribly because I had been involved in a drinking and driving accident. They scrubbed my face roughly with a brush to get all the glass out. Lecturing me the whole time, "Haven't you learned anything after Princess Diana's death"? Which tragically had happened just a few weeks prior.

Crying from the pain, I was trying to explain myself so they'd treat me better. I told them how I always wear my seatbelt, and never drink and drive, which was the truth until now. I also cried because I didn't know Bryan's condition.

They decided that my boot had to come off; it couldn't wait until surgery. The ambulance carrying Lyle and Bryan was taking too long. They had to remove the boot to increase the chances of saving my leg. Again, I screamed and cried, pleading with them to please just put me to sleep and then remove the boot. Thankfully my brain eventually blocked out that excruciating pain.

The ambulance carrying my friends arrived. They were assessed and didn't need surgery. I still didn't know if I was going to live or die, I just wanted to sleep to escape the pain. They told my parents that they did not know if they could save my leg, but that they would do everything they could. I made sure my parents knew that I wanted to donate my organs.

The orthopedic surgeon reattached my foot and a plastic surgeon worked on my face.

After surgery I was admitted to hospital. It was a wait and see game. I didn't want my parents to leave my side. Every time I closed my eyes and drifted off I would wake up in a panic, reliving the accident. On top of the mental anguish, the pain in my leg was severe. Several days later, I was discharged from the hospital.

Once at home, everyone's lives went back to normal. My friends were in school, my dad went back to work and my mom took time off to be with me while I was recovering. The amount of support that I had was phenomenal. The cards, flowers and meals dropped off was amazing. Our community really came together to support us. For the first two to three weeks after I was discharged from the hospital, I stayed home to try and manage the pain. Thankfully home care came in to care for my wounds. Even though I had friends coming over to visit, I was going stir crazy. I needed to get out and experience normal life again. I had friends come and take me out in my wheelchair just to get fresh air, hang out and keep me included in things as much as they could.

After three weeks at home, I decided to go back to school. Between physiotherapy and pain, I was able to attend only a few classes a week. It was nice to be out and socializing with my peers once again. It seemed as though I was getting back to being my old self, at least on the outside. On the inside I was sad. It wasn't until days after the accident that I could bring myself to look in a mirror and when I did, all I could do is cry. That wasn't me staring back! My face was disfigured as far as I was concerned. The scars were not a part of me. I realized that I would never again look the way I had prior to all of this.

My peers were preparing and fundraising for our trip to Louisiana. They were also finalizing all of our graduation plans. I was going to physiotherapy. It was so intense the pain nauseated me and I wanted to give up. But I had one goal in mind and that was to walk at my graduation. Nothing was going to stop that from happening. I persevered and made it through months and months of therapy.

As the weeks went by I was getting less phone calls and less visitors. Everyone was getting on with their lives while I felt that my life was at a standstill. I did try to become a normal teenager again and go to as many parties and activities as I could. But it was never the same. I wasn't the old Chauna anymore. I looked at things completely different since the car accident. I was thankful for being alive, yet sometimes I wondered if it would have been easier if I would have just died that night.

Six short months after the accident, my boyfriend was also in a horrific car accident. I hadn't yet healed from mine and now I was helping him through his. It made me relive my own accident. I was not emotionally strong enough to deal with everything going on, but I pretended to be strong. I was angry that he obviously hadn't learned anything from my bad decision.

Thanks to family and friends, I was able to go on the class trip to Louisiana. They did all the fundraising for me. I was only able to walk for short periods, so my friends and classmates pushed me around in my wheelchair for most of the trip. It was an incredible feeling to be able to attend this once in a lifetime trip. When we returned home we only had a few short weeks until our graduation.

In May 1998 I reached my goal. I was able to walk down the aisle, up the stairs, and onto the stage to receive my grade 12 high school diploma. All the pain, suffering and hard work that I endured with physiotherapy had paid off.

My dream had been to become a registered nurse, but my plans had to change. Instead I went to college to become a medical office assistant. I graduated and received my certificate the following June. This was the beginning of a new chapter for me. I got a job working at a doctor's office and soon after I began my career with the Saskatoon Health Region working in the hospitals. On the outside I looked as though I had healed up perfectly. Unfortunately I was in chronic pain every day of my life.

Over the years the pain in my ankle was getting to be more severe and was playing on me. I had several debridement surgeries on my ankle to try and relieve some of the pain. Finally in 2005 there were no other options for pain relief left. My ankle was bone on bone and I was full of arthritis. I always knew an ankle fusion would probably be in my future but I never really thought that it would come to that.

In December 2005 I had my ankle fused. Although I was no longer able to do some of the things I used to be able to do, I was going to be pain free. Unfortunately the ankle fusion was unsuccessful the first time around, so they had to operate again. I was in a cast and off work for many months.

After the second operation, my depression was worsening. I had no reason to get out of bed in the mornings. I lived alone.

There was nothing I could do but lay around. I decided to get a puppy. I bought a boxer and named her Abbey. She was my saving grace. My boyfriend at this time worked on the road and every time he came home for his days off, he would pack me up and take me to his house for a week. When the week was over, I went back to sitting in my basement suite alone with way too much time to think. Training Abbey was my new focus. I moved in with my boyfriend which had me living closer to my parents and friends.

Eventually the surgery worked and the bones in my ankle successfully united. I was pain free for the first time in 8 years. I went on to live my life as normally as I could. I could finally go back to work.

My greatest joys arrived in April 2007, when I gave birth to my first daughter, and in May 2011, when my second daughter was born.

I started having pain again in 2012. This time it was in my hind foot/heel. Apparently this was common for people who have had ankle fusions. Compensating for the lack of range of motion, the other joints in the body become affected. I had worn out my heel. I tried living like this for as long as possible, but in September 2013 I had a surgery to fuse my heel.

This recovery was different than any of the others in the previous years because this time I had two little girls who needed their mom. I had to get help in to care for them. It was hard for me to do all the necessary mom tasks while I was in a cast and on crutches. I had to depend on others to help me with everything, and I felt like I was not only missing out on my children's lives, but that mine was also on hold. I was supposed to be in a cast for only eight weeks, so my sister took a leave from her job and came to take care of my house and children. Unfortunately things weren't that cut and dry. Again, my bones would not fuse. This meant another surgery.

When the doctor took my cast off to put me in a boot, my incision didn't look right. It looked as though I had an infection. The doctor put me on oral antibiotics in the hopes that my heel would fuse on its own. I continued on the oral antibiotics but my incision area was not looking any better.

My boyfriend and I got engaged in November of 2013. I was still in a cast but we planned our wedding for August in the hopes that I would be healed by then. We got married in August 2014, I was still in a walking cast.

My husband and I went to Jamaica after our wedding. I had been feeling unwell for months, always exhausted. I felt like this for so long that I was beginning to think it was just normal. My incision still looked horrible, as though there was still infection brewing in there.

My husband was away a lot for work so I still had to have a nanny. Someone to take care of the kids, cook and clean. The stress of finding a good nanny and going through so many of them was awful. It played on my mental health and on my poor children.

In an attempt to keep trying to fix and fuse my heel, I had two more surgeries. Each attempt they used different hardware – bigger and stronger. At one point after the second attempt, I had a screw work its way out of my bones right through my skin. The third attempt was the last attempt. They used a hindfoot nail that is about 9 inches long which goes up through the bottom of the foot, up into your leg bones. My very sick self, got even worse. My foot and leg were producing big cyst type pouches full of puss. My skin would burst and puss would run out. I was still taking the same oral antibiotic that I was given over a year before. I reached my lowest point. I was running out of fight. There were a lot of moments I felt like giving up. There were a lot of moments where I went back to thinking that maybe it would have been easier if I would've died in the accident.

Just when I thought I couldn't handle more, I was admitted to hospital with sepsis and osteomyelitis (infection in bone).

In November 2014 I had a CT scan and MRI. Results showed that my osteomyelitis was so severe that the bones in my foot and several inches up my leg were full of holes and looked like a sponge. The infection had spread and worsened. I had a total breakdown. I just couldn't believe that after everything I had been through we were back at square one.

This was the first time the word amputation was used. That word hit me like a ton of bricks. I felt hurt, angry, bitter and robbed. I had fought long and hard... only to lose my leg. I was so sick that I had no choice. It was clear that the infection was not improving. The damage was done and the bone was dead. On top of this, I lost my beloved companion, my dog Abbey. I hit a new emotional low. My two daughters and two stepsons made giving up not an option.

I was scheduled for a below knee amputation on October 7, 2015. The mental toll of going into this surgery was incredible. I couldn't imagine losing my leg. The morning of my surgery, my daughters who were four and eight at the time, signed my leg for the very last time. They were always first to sign or draw on my cast, and they were the last to write on the limb that I was about to lose. When I woke from surgery, I didn't even want to look down. I tried wiggling my toes (something I did out of habit) and I couldn't. I couldn't fathom how life was going to be.

Frustrating years followed with more surgeries on my stump, and problems with a wearing a prosthetic.

I also had one more hurdle to jump, getting off of the painkillers that I had been using to control the pain for the past 2 years. There were resources out there to help me, but I decided to do it on my own. I started by decreasing and then discontinued. Weaning off of opioids is not a fun task. Once I was a at a low dose, I quit cold turkey. I was so sick. I was nauseous, had headaches, was grouchy and I was irritable. I slept for two days while my mom looked after the house and the kids for me. When I woke up, I was clear headed and felt so much better.

I wouldn't have been able to get through this ordeal without the support of my husband, parents, the incredible amputation survivors that I met online, and my friends (you learn who your TRUE friends are.)

I finally got to wear my prosthetic again in November 2017. Occasionally I still need pain killers to get through any length of time using my leg. I decided not to do intense physiotherapy so that I can focus on being a mom. The fact that there is limited tissue available to cover my bone, means that if things change, my next option is an above knee amputation. In my mind, another surgery is not an option, let alone an above knee.

I am starting to get back into a groove. I am still trying to discover and define my new 'normal.' After everything I have been through I have realized that the support of family and friends can get me through anything. The love I have for my children has given me the strength to continue on. The fear I feel about my future lessens with their love, and gives me courage to face it, and to deal with it.

I still have guilt and anger about my leg robbing me of precious time and memories over the last twenty years. Especially lost time with my kids and husband. I had twenty-two surgeries on my leg. Eight of which have been since September 2013.

It kills me to think that I have not been the mom that I always dreamt I would be. That my husband missed out on me being the wife that I had intended to be. I do find comfort in knowing that my children have grown and learned valuable life lessons because of my ordeal. I'm happy that finally my family can see this better me. In hindsight, maybe amputating my leg years ago would have been the best thing, but deep down, I know I would not have been okay waking up from surgery at seventeen without a leg.

Today at 38 years old, I still have trouble seeing photos of myself with no leg. In my mind, that's not me. I look down every day and see it missing. I go as far as cropping my legs out of photos.

There are many things that change once you lose a limb. Things no one thinks about or can comprehend unless you have experienced it. When I wake up the very first thing that comes to mind is "Shit. I don't have a leg." There is no hopping out of bed quickly. If the kids wake up sick, I can't get to them as fast. When I have the stomach flu, I have to either camp out on the bathroom floor or use a bucket. I shower with a chair. When we go anywhere, I have to remember to find out if there is a bathtub, because if there isn't, I need to make other arrangements. Getting dressed is a long process – lots of standing and sitting, hopping off and on the bed. If I decide to change my shoes, I have to allow extra time for that. At times I need assistance getting a shoe on my prosthetic foot. I have to wash my liner every night before bed. I have always been too lazy to take the extra time to wash my face at night and now I have to wash this liner with soap and water every single night. I stand and hop on one leg a lot.

It never fails that as soon as my prosthetic is off, I realize I forgot to get something or do something. I'm now starting to suffer from hip and back problems. I can't ride bikes or go for walks with my kids, go swimming or water sliding (I am hoping to get a waterproof leg soon.) I can't feel if I'm about to slip on ice, trip on something or even step on my cats. I have to carry a bag that contains 'leg supplies' everywhere I go. Walking on sand or any uneven ground is nearly impossible, I can't walk long distances or stand for any length of time. Those are only a few out of the many things I can no longer do.

I chose life over limb so my children would have a mom, and my husband a wife. My leg (or lack thereof) determines what I can or can't do every single day. The adjustments that I have had to make in my everyday life are hard... but I still have my life and for this, I am fortunate. Every year on October 5, my parents have a celebration of my life. This past October marked the 20th anniversary.

If there is any good that has come out of this tragedy it is that I am now stronger. Although it's hard to understand while it's happening, I believe everything happens for a reason. I think my 'reason' for being here today is to speak to youth about the dangers of drinking and driving. I made a mistake that night, getting into a car with an intoxicated driver, but if my story, my struggle, can stop even one person from making the same mistake... my faltering walk will be redeemed.

Chauna Welder Leek lives in rural Saskatchewan with her husband Steve, her two daughters Kamryn and Aidyn, and her two stepsons, Samual and Benjamin.

Following her high school graduation, Chauna attended business college where she obtained her Medical Office Assistant certificate. She began working in the local hospitals. After years of working in many different departments, she found her passion working in Mental Health and Addiction Services.

In Chauna's spare time, she loves traveling, camping, flower gardening and snowmobiling. In the near future, she would like to begin traveling to schools to speak about the dangers of impaired driving.

CONGRATULATIONS
to all our Authors

We are proud to announce that the first three volumes of The Sisterhood *f*olios have all reached

#1 International Best Seller

status in their categories on Amazon.

We have helped 44 authors call themselves #1 International Best Selling Author.

Thank you for sharing your stories, enjoy your well earned status.

The Sisterhood *f*olios:

Live Out Loud

Ignite Your Inner Warrior

Born to be Me

Rebel Rising (June 2018 release